JOHNSON AGONISTES
&
OTHER ESSAYS

Johnson Agonistes

and

Other Essays

By

BERTRAND H. BRONSON

UNIVERSITY OF CALIFORNIA PRESS

Berkeley and Los Angeles

1965

NOTE

The first three essays originally appeared in the *University of California Publications in English* (Volume 3, No. 9), published by the University of California Press in 1944. Cambridge University Press published a clothbound edition, entitled *Johnson Agonistes and Other Essays*, in 1946. All rights reserved. The essay, 'The Double Tradition of Dr. Johnson', was first published in *ELH, A Journal of English Literary History*, June, 1951. Permission to reprint it here is gratefully acknowledged.

FIRST CALIFORNIA PAPER-BOUND EDITION, 1965
PRINTED IN THE UNITED STATES OF AMERICA

CONTENTS

JOHNSON AGONISTES

I. 'EXPOSITION'

Informed that Mrs Montagu, Queen of the Blues, First
of Literary Women, was coming to dine at the Thrales',
Dr Johnson, then approaching 70, began to seesaw with
suppressed mirth. Finally he turned to his new favourite,
the 26-year-old authoress of a recent best seller called
Evelina, and burst out with animation:

'Down with her, Burney!—down with her!—spare her not!—
attack her, fight her, and down with her at once! You are a rising
wit, and she is at the top; and when I was beginning the world, and
was nothing and nobody, the joy of my life was to fire at all the
established wits...to vanquish the great ones was all the delight of
my poor little dear soul! So at her, Burney,—at her, and down with
her!'...

'Miss Burney,' cried Mr Thrale, 'you must get up your courage
for this encounter! I think you should begin with Miss Gregory;
and down with her first.' Dr Johnson: 'No, no, always fly at the
eagle!'[1]

The playful mood should not blind us to the truth of
Johnson's remark about himself. The incomparable fullness and vitality of Boswell's portrait of him for the last
twenty years of his life dims in the reader's mind those
earlier indications of a violent youth who had to shoulder
his way to recognition. But the lines of the sketches are
right, and need only to be scrutinized. We may disregard
if we will the legend of the infant who beat his nurse for
following him too solicitously; but there is no doubting
a later anecdote. When Boswell reminded Johnson that
he had had the reputation while at the University of being
a frolicsome fellow, the Doctor's answer was:

Ah, Sir, I was mad and violent. It was bitterness which they
mistook for frolick. I was miserably poor, and I thought to fight

---

[1] *Diary and Letters of Madame D'Arblay*, ed. Austin Dobson, 1904,
I, 115, 117.

my way by my literature and my wit; so I disregarded all power and all authority.[1]

Mad, violent, and bitter; miserably poor, and conscious of intellectual abilities of a high order, yet unrecognized: the mixture spells, as always, Radical, Iconoclast, Enemy of the Established Order.

But we have to add another characteristic, the presence of which makes combustion even more probable: aggressive physical courage. Johnson, we are told, used to call a man who was afraid of anything 'a scoundrel'. *Scoundrel* was a word he used with surprising readiness (anyone who went to bed before twelve o'clock was also a scoundrel); but in relation to courage he acted as if he meant it literally. Numerous and familiar are the stories of his own hardihood. While writing of the retort to Macpherson, itself an act of courage in the face of Macpherson's size and impudence ('Any violence offered me I shall do my best to repel...I hope I shall never be deterred from detecting what I think a cheat, by the menaces of a ruffian'), Boswell mentions several occasions on which Johnson showed not merely bravery, but even foolhardiness. Thus, when swimming with his young friend Langton at Oxford, he was warned that a certain pool in the river was especially dangerous: he swam straight into it. Told of the danger of a gun's bursting if loaded with several balls, he promptly put in half a dozen and fired it off. Attacked by a gang of four men, at night, in a London street, he 'kept them all at bay, till the watch came up'.[2]

This physical courage, as Boswell suggests, was entirely irrational and instinctive; and it was imperious enough to obliterate for the moment his dread of death. In

---

[1] Boswell, *Life of Johnson*, i, 73–74. The references throughout are to the Hill-Powell edition, Oxford, 1934.

[2] *Life*, ii, 299.

the examples cited, the chance of death is wantonly courted, not for a principle but simply for a whim. And yet the fear of death, as we all know, sat ever upon his mind.

'Mad and violent', he called himself; and Boswell is right in more departments than that of meat and drink when he declares that 'Johnson, though he could be rigidly *abstemious*, was not a *temperate* man'. Violence is often as apparent in total abstention as in headlong luxury; and the pattern of Johnson's temperament, far from being cut to fit the classical Golden Mean, tended everywhere to the volcanic. From his father, he once told Boswell, he had inherited 'a vile melancholy', which made him 'mad all his life, at least not sober'.[1]

Wherever it came from, it is this yeast of insobriety in him that, to an ear sensitive to overtones, makes his expression of even the merest truisms exciting. Taine, who had for the English music decidedly the dull ear of a foreigner, simply yawned: 'Whatever the work', he declared, Johnson 'always writes in the same style... Classical prose attains its perfection in him...Art cannot be more finished, or nature more forced. No one has confined ideas in more strait compartments; none has given stronger relief to dissertation and proof...none has more generally mutilated the flowing liberty of conversation and life by antitheses and technical words....'[2] We may wonder at an implied definition of the classical which, instead of requiring an appropriate dress for the thought, admits the most general mutilation of the 'flowing liberty of conversation and life' to be the perfection of classical prose. But a glimmer of truth lurks in Taine's observa-

[1] *Journal of a Tour to the Hebrides*, ed. R. W. Chapman, Oxford, 1930, p. 302; *Life*, i, 35.
[2] Taine, *Histoire de la littérature anglaise*, Bk. iii, chap. 6 (trans. H. van Laun; New York, 1925, iii, 322–323).

tions: Johnson does almost always forcibly impose his pressure on what he says or writes. The swing of his phrases, even in trivialities, starts from the hips. His mere impatience is another man's passion. Who else would express a momentary irritation at a bashful beauty's silence with a force like this?—

She says nothing, Sir; a talking blackamoor were better than a white creature who adds nothing to life, and by sitting down before one thus desperately silent, takes away the confidence one should have in the company of her chair if she were once out of it.[1]

That is, precisely, to break a butterfly upon a wheel; but an engine with this power does not easily limit itself to flapping bugs. In other words, it is not that the little fishes out of some absurd pomposity talk like whales, but rather that whales cannot simply be whittled down to little fishes. It is all a matter of the amount of energy demanding release.

'Every thing about his character and manners', Boswell has written, 'was forcible and violent.'[2] When, at twenty-six, Johnson married a widow of forty-six, he did so not in the passive desire of being mothered and dominated— though psychologists will shake their heads and ponder. He went to church in that resolute frame of mind of which he was to make such unforgettable report:

Sir, she had read the old romances, and had got into her head the fantastical notion that a woman of spirit should use her lover like a dog. So, Sir, at first she told me that I rode too fast, and she could not keep up with me [—they were both on horseback—]; and, when I rode a little slower, she passed me, and complained that I lagged behind. I was not to be made the slave of caprice; and I resolved to begin as I meant to end. I therefore pushed on briskly, till I was fairly out of her sight. The road lay between two hedges, so I was sure she could not miss it; and I contrived that she should

[1] *Johnsonian Miscellanies*, ed. Hill, I, 289 (Mrs Thrale's *Anecdotes*).
[2] *Life*, IV, 72.

soon come up with me. When she did, I observed her to be in tears.[1]

If Mrs Johnson had read romances, Johnson knew Shakespeare's *Taming of the Shrew*.

Shakespeare, in fact, he did not merely '*know*': he *lived* the scenes, tragic as well as comic. No critic has made stronger confession of the impact of the dramatist upon his imagination. 'He that peruses Shakespeare,' he writes of the murder scene in *Macbeth*, 'looks round alarmed, and starts to find himself alone.' 'I was many years ago so shocked by *Cordelia's* death, that I know not whether I ever endured to read again the last scenes of the play till I undertook to revise them as an editor.'[2] And has any other editor been driven to an outburst like the following, which concerns Desdemona's murder?—'I am glad that I have ended my revisal of this dreadful scene. It is not to be endured.' Of the strength of Johnson's imagination, and of the significance of his lifelong effort to hold it in check, a brilliant study has recently been published.[3] All that need be said at present is that it was no faculty of a 'harmless drudge', but the boiling, turbulent imagination of a poet capable of fine frenzy. All Johnson's most characteristic utterances, oral or written, display this fundamentally imaginative quality, this need for *poiesis*, seeking always the vivid metaphor or simile, the telling word. His very habit of writing, the impatient discharge of a task, galvanized by a single explosive impulse, reveals the same truth. But his emotions had staying power as well:

Once, indeed, (said he,) I was disobedient; I refused to attend my father to Uttoxeter-market. Pride was the source of that refusal,

---

[1] *Life*, I, 96.
[2] *Works*, Oxford, 1825, VI, 71 and 175. All references to Johnson's works, unless otherwise noted, are to this edition.
[3] W. B. C. Watkins, *Perilous Balance*, Princeton, 1939.

and the remembrance of it was painful. A few years ago, I desired to atone for this fault; I went to Uttoxeter in very bad weather, and stood for a considerable time bareheaded in the rain, on the spot where my father's stall used to stand. In contrition I stood, and I hope the penance was expiatory.[1]

If, indeed, Johnson ever, as his enemies supposed, set up for Sir Oracle, it was not by composing his demeanour into a wilful stillness. What drew him, in part, to Boswell was the latter's avid curiosity and zest for fresh experience. And when occasion offered, though at the age of sixty-four, he set out with him on an arduous junket through the wilderness.

> Why should a man, whose blood is warm within,
> Sit like his grandsire cut in alabaster?

In the last months of his life, hopeless of recovery from fatal sickness, 'such', says Boswell, 'was his intellectual ardour...that he said to one friend, "Sir, I look upon every day to be lost, in which I do not make a new acquaintance"; and to another, when talking of his illness, "I will be conquered; I will not capitulate".'[2]

Examples could be multiplied without end in illustration of the ferment and tumult of Johnson's nature. Are we, then, to conclude that habitually we think mistakenly of him? Was he really a firebrand needing only to be tossed among dry fagots to start a conflagration? The query has only to be phrased to be denied. What we have seen so far is indeed the disposition of a man who will swim instinctively against the current, whose forces are naturally called into play by opposition and difficulty. Of such temperaments revolutionaries are made: so much is clear. But when Johnson is brought to the bar on any of the fundamental issues, he ranges himself on the conservative

---

[1] *Life*, iv, 373.　　　　　　[2] *Life*, iv, 374.

side. Authority, and more authority, is what he wants, in Religion, in Morals, in Politics, in Literature. To labour the general truth would be more than ungrateful; it is too obvious and well known. The orthodoxy of his religious opinions is one of the most striking features of his character. In politics, it is not yet forgotten in America that he wrote *Taxation No Tyranny*. One brief paragraph in this pamphlet contains, according to Leslie Stephen, his whole political theory. The paragraph is as follows:

> In sovereignty there are no gradations. There may be limited royalty, there may be limited consulship; but there can be no limited government. There must, in every society, be some power or other, from which there is no appeal, which admits no restrictions, which pervades the whole mass of the community, regulates and adjusts all subordination, enacts laws or repeals them, erects or annuls judicatures, extends or contracts privileges, exempt itself from question or control, and bounded only by physical necessity.[1]

This simple fundamental tenet Johnson illustrated conversationally in various sallies, and by implication or argument in his political tracts. There could hardly be a plainer declaration of belief in the authoritarian principle.

> By this power, wherever it subsists [he continues], all legislation and jurisdiction is animated and maintained. From this all legal rights are emanations, which, whether equitably or not, may be legally recalled. It is not infallible, for it may do wrong; but it is irresistible, for it can be resisted only by rebellion, by an act which makes it questionable, what shall be thenceforward the supreme power.[2]

Hence the Whigs and 'patriots' and 'democrats' of his day get short shrift, because they in their several ways deny the supremacy of any such authority and bring chaos in their train. 'Whiggism, at the time of the Revolution,

---

[1] *Works*, VI, 234. [2] *Works*, VI, 234–235.

he said, was accompanied with certain principles; but latterly, as a mere party distinction under Walpole and the Pelhams, was no better than the politicks of stock-jobbers, and the religion of infidels.'[1] Johnson thought, as did George III himself, that the king ought to have more power rather than less, and, given ability and integrity, should be in a sense his own minister, 'the directing soul and spirit of his administration'.[2]

Johnson's conservatism, therefore, though not Toryism in the narrow party sense of the word, was a matter of deep-lying convictions. In morals, it drove him to ask a rule for right and wrong, 'in their abstracted and invariable state, divested of the prejudices of age and country'. In poetry, it made him 'neglect the minuter discriminations...for those characteristicks which are alike obvious to vigilance and carelessness':[3] it made him prefer, in fiction, 'characters of nature' to 'characters of manners'.

II. 'DEVELOPMENT'

The opposition of these two forces, the conservatism of intellectual attitude and the ebullient temperament, is at the root of most of his inconsistencies, and is perpetually fascinating. It keeps him from ever being a philosopher in the strictest sense, although his powerful intellect was as firm in its grasp of a logical concatenation as it was prone to generalize. Philosophy was too narrow a room for his humanity: he could not look upon a metaphysical system, no matter how pretty the structure, as a desirable exchange for the rich irrelevancies and contradictions by which men live. Hence his notorious opinion of Berkeley and Hume. Generalization, yes; metaphysical abstraction, no. Confronted with a system, he always tries it with a

---

[1] *Life*, II, 117 (Dr Maxwell's *Collectanea*). [2] *Ibid*.
[3] *Rasselas*, chap. x.

8

pragmatic ear; and if the vibrations set up a beat, the system is out of tune:

> The bigot of philosophy...is entangled in systems by which truth and falsehood are inextricably complicated, or undertakes to talk on subjects which nature did not form him able to comprehend. The Cartesian, who denies that his horse feels the spur, or that the hare is afraid when the hounds approach her; the disciple of Malbranche, who maintains that the man was not hurt by the bullet, which, according to vulgar apprehension, swept away his legs; the follower of Berkeley, who while he sits writing at his table, declares that he has neither table, paper, nor fingers; have all the honour at least of being deceived by fallacies not easily detected, and may plead that they did not forsake truth, but for appearances which they were not able to distinguish from it.[1]

Thus, during the years when we know him best, the subtleties of metaphysics had come to seem to him a mere game of paradoxes, without any roots in experience, which any man might play who had nothing more important to do. But, though intellectual paradoxes were abhorrent to him on principle, he was never beyond the temptation of them in conversation, when his instinct to oppose had led him into a tight corner; and often he could not resist the sheer fun of seeing what could be said in favour of an untenable position.

For the present purpose, it will be obvious that our terminology need not be confined to any rigorous definition. It was said earlier that he had the disposition of the subverter, the radical. The objection might be raised, that proof was still to seek. It is true that specific evidence to justify the application of such terms is scanty; and so far as is known he seldom allowed the temperament to lead him beyond argument into act. George Steevens tells an anecdote of his provoking a riot at 'Marybone' Gardens which might provide a solitary but strikingly characteristic

---

[1] *The Idler*, No. 10, *Works*, IV, 179.

exception. His curiosity had been aroused by talk of Torré's fireworks there, and he went with Steevens to watch the display.

The evening had proved showery; and soon after the few people present were assembled, publick notice was given, that the conductors to the wheels, suns, stars, etc. were so thoroughly watersoaked, that it was impossible any part of the exhibition should be made. 'This is a mere excuse, (says the Doctor,) to save their crackers for a more profitable company. Let us but hold up our sticks, and threaten to break those coloured lamps that surround the Orchestra, and we shall soon have our wishes gratified. The core of the fireworks cannot be injured; let the different pieces be touched in their respective centers, and they will do their offices as well as ever.'—Some young men who overheard him, immediately began the violence he had recommended, and an attempt was speedily made to fire some of the wheels which appeared to have received the smallest damage; but to little purpose were they lighted, for most of them completely failed.—The authour of 'The Rambler', however, may be considered on this occasion, as the ringleader of a successful riot, though not as a skilful pyrotechnist.[1]

But at least one glimpse of the young intellectual radical is on record in his own words. Talking impatiently in later years of those, like Rousseau, who were led into paradox 'by a childish desire of novelty'—innovators who, finding that Truth was a 'cow that would yield no more milk, were gone to milk the bull'—he declared:

When I was a boy, I used always to choose the wrong side of a debate, because most ingenious things, that is to say, most new things, could be said upon it.

And he proceeded at once to give an example of the technique:

Sir, there is nothing for which you may not muster up more plausible arguments, than those which are urged against wealth and other external advantages. Why now, there is stealing; why should it be thought a crime? When we consider by what unjust methods property has been often acquired, and that what was unjustly got

[1] *Life*, IV, 324.

it must be unjust to keep, where is the harm in one man's taking the property of another from him? Besides, Sir, when we consider the bad use that many people make of their property, and how much better use the thief may make of it, it may be defended as a very allowable practice.... When I was running about this town a very poor fellow, I was a great arguer for the advantages of poverty; but I was, at the same time, very sorry to be poor. Sir, all the arguments which are brought to represent poverty as no evil, shew it to be evidently a great evil. You never find people labouring to convince you that you may live very happily upon a plentiful fortune.[1]

Praise of poverty is hard to find in Johnson's printed works; but a glorified poverty enters the poem which he wrote when he was feeling the pinch of want most acutely. Throughout *London* the implication is that only the poor are honest and deserving, that 'starving merit' is the only merit to be found, and that virtue left England when wealth encroached upon simpler society. Some of these sentiments are borrowed from the Juvenalian original; but personal miseries weight the lines:

> This mournful truth is ev'rywhere confess'd,
> Slow rises worth, by poverty depress'd....
> Then through the world a wretched vagrant roam,
> For where can starving merit find a home?
> In vain your mournful narrative disclose,
> While all neglect, and most insult your woes.[2]

Bitterness was not surprising in one who had nearly starved for a year in face of the insensibility of a great city, and even been arrested for debt. Yet Johnson afterwards told Sir Joshua Reynolds of a night he particularly remembered, when he and Savage walked round and round St James's Square for lack of lodging, not at all depressed, 'but in high spirits and brimful of patriotism', inveighing against the government and resolved to 'stand by their country'.[3]

[1] *Life*, I, 441.   [2] *London*, ll. 176–177, 190–193.
[3] *Life*, I, 164.

These violent political sentiments, also, pervade the *London*, one of the chief receptacles of Johnson's anti-Walpolian fury:

> Here let those reign, whom pensions can incite
> To vote a patriot black, a courtier white;
> Explain their country's dear-bought rights away,
> And plead for pirates in the face of day;
> With slavish tenets taint our poison'd youth,
> And lend a lie the confidence of truth.
>
> Let such raise palaces, and manors buy,
> Collect a tax, or farm a lottery;
> With warbling eunuchs fill a licens'd stage,
> And lull to servitude a thoughtless age....
>
> Scarce can our fields, such crowds at Tyburn die,
> With hemp the gallows and the fleet supply.
> Propose your schemes, ye senatorian band,
> Whose ways and means support the sinking land:
> Lest ropes be wanting in the tempting spring,
> To rig another convoy for the king.[1]

Familiar enough is Johnson's remark that, in writing up the Parliamentary Debates in 1739–1741, he took care 'not to let the Whig dogs have the best of it'. Not so familiar is his *Marmor Norfolciense*, a pamphlet published anonymously in 1739, written to throw contempt upon Walpole, George II and his house, and their policies and measures. The tone is heavily ironic. Announcement is made of the discovery in a Norfolk field (Walpole's estate) of an ancient stone rudely inscribed with a Latin prophecy, which the author proceeds to interpret with covert insinuations applying to the present. The whole thing is, of course, a Swiftian hoax. After allusions to the discord following upon the Hanoverian succession, and to the consequent flourishing of the French lilies, to the timidity of the British lion and the profligacy of Walpole and the

---

[1] *London*, ll. 51–60, 242–247.

King, he carries his ironic attack to the following perilous
length, upon the lines

> And, yet more strange! his [the lion's] veins
> a horse shall drain,
> Nor shall the passive coward once complain!

Were I to proceed in the same tenour of interpretation, by which
I explained the moon and the lilies, I might observe, that a horse is
the arms of H[anover]. But how, then, does the horse suck the
lion's blood! Money is the blood of the body politick.—But my zeal
for the present happy establishment will not suffer me to pursue a
train of thought, that leads to such shocking conclusions. The idea
is detestable, and such as, it ought to be hoped, can enter into the
mind of none but a virulent republican, or bloody jacobite. There is
not one honest man in the nation unconvinced, how weak an
attempt it would be to endeavour to confute this insinuation; an
insinuation which no party will dare to abet, and of so fatal and
destructive a tendency, that it may prove equally dangerous to the
author, whether true or false.[1]

He therefore gives over the attempt to interpret the in-
scription correctly and recommends for that purpose the
formation of a committee of thirty, drawn equally from the
Law and the Army, whose qualifications he describes with
great vigour:

It is well known to be the constant study of the lawyers to discover, in acts of parliament, meanings which escaped the committees
that drew them up, and the senates that passed them into laws, and
to explain wills, into a sense wholly contrary to the intention of the
testator. How easily may an adept in these admirable and useful arts,
penetrate into the most hidden import of this prediction? A man,
accustomed to satisfy himself with the obvious and natural meaning
of a sentence, does not easily shake off his habit; but a true-bred
lawyer never contents himself with one sense, when there is another
to be found.[2]

For the army, the darling of the martinet George II, he
has equal scorn. They, having so much leisure to become

---

[1] *Works*, vi, 105.   [2] *Works*, vi, 109.

pretty men, may polish the lawyers' obscure style of expression:

> There may not, perhaps, be found in the army such a number of men, who have ever condescended to pass through the labours, and irksome forms of education in use, among the lower classes of people, or submitted to learn the mercantile and plebeian arts of writing and reading. I must own, that though I entirely agree with the notions of the uselessness of any such trivial accomplishments in the military profession, and of their inconsistency with more valuable attainments; though I am convinced, that a man who can read and write becomes, at least, a very disagreeable companion to his brother soldiers, if he does not absolutely shun their acquaintance; that he is apt to imbibe, from his books, odd notions of liberty and independency, and even, sometimes, of morality and virtue, utterly inconsistent with the desirable character of a pretty gentleman; though writing frequently stains the whitest finger, and reading has a natural tendency to cloud the aspect, and depress that airy and thoughtless vivacity, which is the distinguishing characteristick of a modern warriour; yet, on this single occasion, I cannot but heartily wish, that, by a strict search, there may be discovered, in the army, fifteen men who can write and read.[1]

Greenwich Hospital, he suggests, will make a good residence for this group of experts; and if the new buildings should not be ready in time,

> it will be necessary to make room for their reception, by the expulsion of such of the seamen as have no pretensions to the settlement there, but fractured limbs, loss of eyes, or decayed constitutions, who have lately been admitted in such numbers, that it is now scarce possible to accommodate a nobleman's groom, footman, or postilion, in a manner suitable to the dignity of his profession, and the original design of the foundation.[2]

He calculates the cost of the enterprise at a moderate £2000 annual salary for each professor, £30,000 'for the support of the publick table', £40,000 for secret service; so that success may be achieved in five years or so,

> without burdening the publick with more than £650,000 which may be paid out of the sinking fund; or, if it be not thought proper

[1] *Works*, VI, 110–111. [2] *Works*, VI, 112.

to violate that sacred treasure, by...a general poll-tax, or excise upon bread.[1]

This was the Johnson who a little later was to sit moodily in Chesterfield's 'outer rooms', waiting for admittance to the great man's presence, while he formulated fuliginous definitions of patrons and patronage and confirmed his resolve to be independent though he should starve. Boswell denies Sir John Hawkins's story, that warrants were issued by the government for Johnson's arrest upon the publication of *Marmor Norfolciense*, and that he lay for a while concealed in Lambeth Marsh. But Hawkins had known Johnson in those earlier days, and Boswell's denial is based on the mere fact that he had been unable to find any record of such a warrant in the offices of government. There would be nothing very surprising if an attempt had been made to apprehend him for so incendiary an attack.

Almost equally sulphurous is another pamphlet of the same year, 1739, after the passage of the Licensing Act, and consequent upon the refusal of Brooke's *Gustavus Vasa* for the stage.[2] This was an ironical vindication of the licensers, professing bewilderment that there should be any objection to their course of action. Poets, it declares, are always affecting to concern themselves with posterity, to the strange disregard of the present ministry; and the contemporary set of poets is especially obnoxious to government. This curious distemper, under which such people suffer,

is almost always complicated with ideas of the high prerogatives of human nature, of a sacred unalienable birthright, which no man has conferred upon us, and which neither kings can take, nor senates give away; which we may justly assert whenever and by whom-

[1] *Works*, vi, 112–113.
[2] 'A Complete Vindication of the Licensers of the Stage, from the Malicious and Scandalous Aspersions of Mr Brooke,' etc.

soever it is attacked; and which, if ever it should happen to be lost, we may take the first opportunity to recover.

The natural consequence of these chimeras is contempt of authority, and an irreverence for any superiority but what is founded upon merit; and their notions of merit are very peculiar, for it is among them no great proof of merit to be wealthy and powerful, to wear a garter or a star, to command a regiment or a senate, to have the ear of the minister or of the king, or to possess any of those virtues and excellencies, which, among us, entitle a man to little less than worship and prostration.[1]

The opinions of this sect, the author ironically continues, are

evidently and demonstrably opposite to that system of subordination and dependence, to which we are indebted for the present tranquillity of the nation, and that cheerfulness and readiness with which the two houses concur in all our designs.... Let me be forgiven if I cannot speak with temper of such insolence as this: is a man without title, pension, or place, to suspect the impartiality or the judgment of those who are entrusted with the administration of publick affairs?[2]

Gustavus, in speaking of his poverty, is made in the rejected play to declare:

> Beyond the sweeping of the proudest train
> That shades a monarch's heel, I prize these weeds;
> For they are sacred to my country's freedom.

Here [says the mock defender] this abandoned son of liberty makes a full discovery of his execrable principles: the tatters of Gustavus, the usual dress of the assertors of these doctrines, are of more divinity, because they are sacred to freedom, than the sumptuous and magnificent robes of regality itself. Such sentiments are truly detestable....

The heel of a monarch, or even the print of his heel, is a thing too venerable and sacred to be treated with such levity, and placed in contrast with rags and poverty. He, that will speak contemptuously of the heel of a monarch, will, whenever he can with security, speak contemptuously of his head.[3]

[1] *Works*, v, 332–333.   [2] *Works*, v, 333.
[3] *Works*, v, 340.

The violence of these attacks on the government Johnson never surpassed. With the fall of Walpole his own
anxiety seems to have subsided. Taught in part by the
mere passage of the 'hypocritic days', he pondered with
increasing conviction the lesson finally expressed in *The
Traveller*, in lines contributed by himself;

> [In every government, though terrors reign,
> Though tyrant kings, or tyrant laws restrain,]
> How small, of all that human hearts endure,
> That part which laws or kings can cause or cure.
> Still to ourselves in every place consign'd,
> Our own felicity we make or find[1] —

a truth which he had by then already worked out with
profound feeling and impressive amplitude in *Rasselas*.

His opinion of the petty politics of the 'forties, with
their increasing timidity and corruption, he expressed in
the contemptuous lines of the *Vanity of Human Wishes*:

> Through Freedom's sons no more remonstrance rings,
> Degrading nobles and controlling kings;
> Our supple tribes repress their patriot throats,
> And ask no questions but the price of votes;
> With weekly libels and septennial ale,
> Their wish is full to riot and to rail.[2]

His general distaste for the position of national affairs
was provoked to fuller expression by the French and
Indian Wars, in an article published in the summer of
1756, *Observations on the State of Affairs*. Here he declares flatly that the dispute between the French and the
English is 'only the quarrel of two robbers for the spoils of
a passenger.... Such [he says] is the contest, that no honest
man can heartily wish success to either party.'[3] But that he
did not believe in a passive acquiescence to authority is
indicated in an earlier sentence of the pamphlet:

For whatever may be urged by ministers, or those whom vanity or
interest make the followers of ministers, concerning the necessity

---

[1] Goldsmith, *The Traveller*, ll. 429–432.
[2] Lines 93–98   [3] *Works*, VI, 114, 115

of confidence in our governours, and the presumption of prying, with profane eyes, into the recesses of policy, it is evident, that this reverence can be claimed only by counsels yet unexecuted, and projects suspended in deliberation.[1]

In another article, published in the same year, he casts an acid eye over the further course of the war and finds little to like, either in past events or future prospects. He was roused to oppose the measure to bring in an army of mercenaries to defend the English coasts from invasion, arguing that a sufficient militia could easily be raised to do the job, and concluding:

I believe, neither our friends nor enemies will think it proper to insult our coasts, when they expect to find upon them a hundred and fifty thousand Englishmen, with swords in their hands.[2]

His eye was on human life rather than on the great manœuvres; and early in the Seven Years' War he wrote two short papers of greater interest to the student of his mind and sympathies. When the French prisoners of war began to flow into the country, they were left for a time almost destitute and unprovided. Then, as their plight began to attract notice and solicit charity, the complaint began to be heard that charity began at home. Johnson wrote an introduction to the report of the committee on relief, in which he answered this objection:

It has been urged, that charity, like other virtues, may be im-properly and unseasonably exerted; that, while we are relieving Frenchmen, there remain many Englishmen unrelieved; that, while we lavish pity on our enemies, we forget the misery of our friends.

Granted this argument all it can prove, and what is the con-clusion?—That to relieve the French is a good action, but that a better may be conceived. This is all the result, and this all is very little. To do the best can seldom be the lot of man: it is sufficient if, when opportunities are presented, he is ready to do good. How little virtue could be practised, if beneficence were to wait always for the most

1 *Works*, VI, 113.
2 'Observations on the Treaties,' etc., *Works*, VI, 147.

proper objects, and the noblest occasions; occasions that may never happen, and objects that may never be found.

The opponents of this charity must allow it to be good, and will not easily prove it not to be the best. That charity is best, of which the consequences are most extensive; the relief of enemies has a tendency to unite mankind in fraternal affection; to soften the acrimony of adverse nations, and dispose them to peace and amity; in the mean time, it alleviates captivity, and takes away something from the miseries of war. The rage of war, however mitigated, will always fill the world with calamity and horrour; let it not, then, be unnecessarily extended; let animosity and hostility cease together; and no man be longer deemed an enemy, than while his sword is drawn against us.[1]

The other paper is on the bravery of the common English soldier. Johnson is pondering the truth that

Our nation may boast, beyond any other people in the world, of a kind of epidemick bravery, diffused equally through all its ranks. We can shew a peasantry of heroes, and fill our armies with clowns, whose courage may vie with that of their general.

Reflecting on this fact, he is moved to try to account for it. It is interesting that he cuts through the common cant about British Freedom and Sons of Liberty to a more restricted and personal explanation. The passage deserves to be quoted:

There are some, perhaps, who would imagine, that every Englishman fights better than the subjects of absolute governments, because he has more to defend. But what has the English more than the French soldier? Property they are both, commonly, without. Liberty is, to the lowest rank of every nation, little more than the choice of working or starving; and this choice is, I suppose, equally allowed in every country. The English soldier seldom has his head very full of the constitution; nor has there been, for more than a century, any war that put the property or liberty of a single Englishman in danger.

Whence, then, is the courage of the English vulgar? It proceeds, in my opinion, from that dissolution of dependence, which obliges every man to regard his own character. While every man is fed by

[1] *Works*, VI, 148–149.

his own hands, he has no need of any servile arts; he may always have wages for his labour; and is no less necessary to his employer, than his employer is to him. While he looks for no protection from others, he is naturally roused to be his own protector; and having nothing to abate his esteem of himself, he, consequently, aspires to the esteem of others. Thus every man that crowds our streets is a man of honour, disdainful of obligation, impatient of reproach, and desirous of extending his reputation among those of his own rank; and, as courage is in most frequent use, the fame of courage is most eagerly pursued. From this neglect of subordination, I do not deny, that some inconveniencies may, from time to time, proceed: the power of the law does not, always, sufficiently supply the want of reverence, or maintain the proper distinction between different ranks; but good and evil will grow up in this world together; and they who complain, in peace, of the insolence of the populace, must remember, that their insolence in peace is bravery in war.[1]

The final sentence, I believe, is the last appearance of equilibrium in Johnson's statements about subordination and independence. Henceforth we shall find the scales tipped always toward the first. In one of the earliest of his conversations with Boswell (June 25, 1763), he declared: 'Sir, I am a friend to subordination, as most conducive to the happiness of society. There is a reciprocal pleasure in governing and being governed.'

His political attitude from this time forward can be fixed with comparative distinctness. Order and stability are the ends to be sought, because they best promote the good of the whole society. Abuses on the part of the governors, individual injustices, are inevitable. They are insignificant and partial evils compared to the ills of a society which is not anchored to a supreme, unchallengeable authority. Ideally, the advantage of a constitutional monarch is that he is this supreme untouchable power, a symbol of abstract right. With this ultimate authority secure, everything that goes on in the practical realm of government may be subject to question. Since what is

[1] *Works*, VI, 151–152.

wrong is not ascribed to majesty, it is not above reach of correction. 'Redress is always to be had against oppression, by punishing the immediate agents.'[1] If a judge condemns a man unjustly, the judge is subject to prosecution, even though the King commanded him to act as he did. The underlying paradox Johnson does not resolve. On the practical level, he treats as supreme the effective legislative power, and grows less and less tolerant of any serious challenge to its authority, even though the abuse of it may be patent. Yet, though he seldom insists upon it, he holds in reserve the consideration, to which Boswell invites attention by italic letters, '*that if the abuse be enormous, Nature will rise up, and claiming her original rights, overturn a corrupt political system*'.[2] This generous sentiment, says Boswell, 'he uttered with great fervour'. Indeed, it is a proviso which goes far to undermine his whole doctrine: no wonder that Boswell marks it 'as a noble instance of that truly dignified spirit of freedom which ever glowed in his heart, though he was charged with slavish tenets by superficial observers; because he was at all times indignant against that false patriotism, that pretended love of freedom, that unruly restlessness, which is inconsistent with the stable authority of any good government'.[3]

To this position, radically self-contradictory but not for that any the less characteristic of the race of man, he adhered to the end of his life. His further utterances on the events of the 'sixties and 'seventies throw into relief the negative side of it. His accepting the royal pension in 1762 laid him open to the malice of petty minds, and derogatory comment was frequent. Boswell, always one for prodding up the larger mammals, mentioned these reflections on his character soon after their first acquaintance, no doubt expecting an explosion.

---

[1] *Life*, I, 424.   [2] *Loc. cit.*   [3] *Loc. cit.*

Why, Sir, (said [Johnson], with a hearty laugh,) it is a mighty foolish noise that they make. I have accepted of a pension as a reward which has been thought due to my literary merit; and now that I have this pension, I am the same man in every respect that I have ever been; I retain the same principles. It is true, that I cannot now curse (smiling) the House of Hanover; nor would it be decent for me to drink King James's health in the wine that King George gives me money to pay for. But, Sir, I think that the pleasure of cursing the House of Hanover, and drinking King James's health, are amply overbalanced by three hundred pounds a year.[1]

'I wish,' he humorously observed some years later, when the same subject arose, 'I wish my pension were twice as large, that they might make twice as much noise.'[2]

The democratic fever over Wilkes's expulsion from the House of Commons, and the American resistance to taxation, called out his most considerable essays in the political field, the papers which have done most to brand him in the eyes of posterity as a die-hard. Violence in political principles, as he once remarked in conversation, is much increased by opposition. 'There was a violent Whig, with whom I used to contend with great eagerness. After his death I felt my Toryism much abated.'[3] *The False Alarm*, Johnson's pamphlet on the Wilkes affair, is a brazen piece of special pleading; but it is probably the most entertaining of all his political tracts, because of the pungency of its invective. Nor is it devoid of general observations permanently valuable. The question whether the House of Commons had exceeded its prerogative in refusing to readmit Wilkes upon his re-election is vigorously and summarily handled by Johnson. Political power, he declares, was originally justified by necessity, and made legal by precedent. Let it be granted that this power may from time to time be oppressively and injuriously exerted.

[1] *Life*, i, 429.   [2] *Loc. cit.*
[3] *Tour to the Hebrides* (Oxford text, ed. R. W. Chapman), p. 421.

The commons must be controlled, or be exempt from control. If they are exempt, they may do injury which cannot be redressed; if they are controlled, they are no longer legislative. If the possibility of abuse be an argument against authority, no authority ever can be established: if the actual abuse destroys its legality, there is no legal government now in the world.... All government supposes subjects; all authority implies obedience: to suppose in one the right to command what another has the right to refuse, is absurd and contradictory; a state, so constituted, must rest for ever in motionless equipoise, with equal attractions of contrary tendency.[1]

He admits that forcible objections may be made to this position; but declares that 'theoretical nicety' is unattainable in political disquisition, because every political institution has developed pragmatically.

Governments formed by chance, and gradually improved by such expedients as the successive discovery of their defects happened to suggest, are never to be tried by a regular theory. They are fabricks of dissimilar materials, raised by different architects, upon different plans. We must be content with them, as they are; should we attempt to mend their disproportions, we might easily demolish, and difficultly rebuild them.[2]

He does not believe that the present excitement is at all commensurate with its cause, nor that those who are making most noise are sound judges of the dispute.

All wrong ought to be rectified. If Mr Wilkes is deprived of a lawful seat, both he and his electors have reason to complain; but it will not be easily found, why, among the innumerable wrongs of which a great part of mankind are hourly complaining, the whole care of the publick should be transferred to Mr Wilkes and the freeholders of Middlesex, who might all sink into nonexistence, without any other effect, than that there would be room made for a new rabble, and a new retailer of sedition and obscenity. The cause of our country would suffer little; the rabble, whencesoever they come, will be always patriots, and always supporters of the bill of rights.[3]

[1] *Works*, VI, 159, 161–162. [2] *Works*, VI, 164.
[3] *Works*, VI, 169.

Comparable irregularities have occurred times without number, Johnson declares,

yet the general state of the nation has continued the same. The sun has risen, and the corn has grown, and, whatever talk has been of the danger of property, yet he that ploughed the field commonly reaped it; and he that built a house was master of the door; the vexation excited by injustice suffered, or supposed to be suffered, by any private man, or single community, was local and temporary....

But quiet and security are now at an end....We not only see events in their causes, but before their causes; we hear the thunder while the sky is clear, and see the mine sprung before it is dug. Political wisdom has, by the force of English genius, been improved, at last, not only to political intuition, but to political prescience... we hear of nothing but of an alarming crisis, of violated rights, and expiring liberties. The morning rises upon new wrongs, and the dreamer passes the night in imaginary shackles.

The sphere of anxiety is now enlarged; he that hitherto cared only for himself, now cares for the publick; for he has learned, that the happiness of individuals is comprised in the prosperity of the whole; and that his country never suffers, but he suffers with it, however it happens that he feels no pain.

Fired with this fever of epidemick patriotism, the tailor slips his thimble, the draper drops his yard, and the blacksmith lays down his hammer; they meet at an honest alehouse, consider the state of the nation, read or hear the last petition, lament the miseries of the time, are alarmed at the dreadful crisis, and subscribe to the support of the bill of rights.[1]

In a pamphlet addressed four years later to the electors of Britain,[2] Johnson amplified his definition of patriots true and false and warned his readers to be on their guard against specious appearances. The brief tract is a useful corrective to prevalent misunderstandings of the famous dictum, 'Patriotism is the last refuge of a scoundrel'. His true meaning, of course, is much closer to 'Scoundrels make a profession of patriotism their last resort'.

Another pamphlet, *Thoughts on the Late Transactions Respecting Falkland's Islands*, published in 1771, is a powerful and considered defence of the Government for

---

[1] *Works*, VI, 170–171.　　　　　[2] *The Patriot* (1774).

resisting the attempts of firebrands to drag the country into war with Spain. It contains a remarkable portrait of Junius, elaborated with rhetorical art and sonority; and an indictment of unnecessary war, which still smoulders in the reading. On historical cause and effect, Johnson generalizes as follows:

It seems to be almost the universal errour of historians to suppose it politically, as it is physically true, that every effect has a proportionate cause. In the inanimate action of matter upon matter, the motion produced can be but equal to the force of the moving power; but the operations of life, whether private or publick, admit no such laws. The caprices of voluntary agents laugh at calculation. It is not always that there is a strong reason for a great event. Obstinacy and flexibility, malignity and kindness, give place, alternately, to each other; and the reason of the vicissitudes, however important may be the consequences, often escapes the mind in which the change is made.[1]

The last of Johnson's political tracts, *Taxation No Tyranny*, though perhaps little read to-day, is yet too well remembered to demand extended notice. It is not so readable as *The False Alarm*, because its form is partly dictated by the congressional resolutions, the points of which Johnson undertakes successively to answer. There are few passages in which he frees himself sufficiently to work up an independent momentum. Yet there are paragraphs of telling impact, and on its own narrow ground the argument is almost unanswerable. Perhaps the most Johnsonian feature appears in the adapting of the congressional resolutions to an imaginary Declaration of Independence by the county of Cornwall.[2] Thereafter, the whole dispute is put succinctly enough:

The argument of the irregular troops of controversy, stripped of its colours, and turned out naked to the view, is no more than this. Liberty is the birthright of man, and where obedience is compelled, there is no liberty. The answer is equally simple. Government is

[1] *Works*, VI, 195.   [2] *Works*, VI, 254–257.

necessary to man, and where obedience is not compelled, there is no government. If the subject refuses to obey, it is the duty of authority to use compulsion. Society cannot subsist but by the power, first of making laws, and then of enforcing them.[1]

With a political philosophy laying such stress upon stability, Johnson's attitude toward hereditary rank is easy to calculate. Its existence, and the acceptance of it, 'tends greatly to human happiness'. It is a 'plain invariable principle' upon which civilized society is settled and agreed, so that there need be no contention for precedence. And inasmuch as it is purely a matter of accident that one is born with such a distinction and another not, there is no reason for jealousy in connection with it. When someone suggested that inner worth ought to be the only distinction between men, Johnson replied:

> Why, Sir, mankind have found that this cannot be. How shall we determine the proportion of intrinsick merit? Were that to be the only distinction amongst mankind, we should soon quarrel about the degrees of it. Were all distinctions abolished, the strongest would not long acquiesce, but would endeavour to obtain a superiority by their bodily strength....Were we all upon an equality, we should have no other enjoyment than mere animal pleasure.[2]

Against all who complained of the inequity of these fortuitous distinctions, Johnson stoutly maintained that levellers were hypocrites motivated by selfishness. He confuted the democratic professions of Mrs Macaulay by acquiescing to her doctrine and then proposing at her table that her footman be given a place with the guests. 'She has never liked me since', he declared. 'Sir, your levellers wish to level down as far as themselves; but they cannot bear levelling up to themselves. They would all have some people under them; why not then have some people above them?'[3] He would try a certain author who

---

[1] *Works*, VI, 257.   [2] *Life*, I, 442.
[3] *Life*, I, 447–448.

showed no deference to rank with a similar practical experiment:

'Suppose a shoemaker should claim an equality with him, as he does with a Lord; how he would stare. "Why, Sir, do you stare? (says the shoemaker,) I do great service to society. 'Tis true I am paid for doing it; but so are you, Sir: and I am sorry to say it, paid better than I am, for doing something not so necessary. For mankind could do better without your books, than without my shoes." Thus, Sir, there would be a perpetual struggle for precedence.'[1]

With greater severity he censured the whole class of democrats who acted what they professed. 'The quiet of the nation', he wrote in *The False Alarm*,

has been, for years, disturbed by a faction, against which all factions ought to conspire; for its original principle is the desire of leveling; it is only animated, under the name of zeal, by the natural malignity of the mean against the great....

The whole conduct of this despicable faction is distinguished by plebeian grossness, and savage indecency....An infallible characteristick of meanness is cruelty. This is the only faction, that has shouted at the condemnation of a criminal, and that, when his innocence procured his pardon, has clamoured for his blood.

All other parties, however enraged at each other, have agreed to treat the throne with decency; but these low-born railers have attacked not only the authority, but the character of their sovereign, and have endeavoured, surely without effect, to alienate the affections of the people from the only king, who, for almost a century, has much appeared to desire, or much endeavoured to deserve them.[2]

For the philosophers who underpropped such insubordination as this, Johnson had, of course, the keenest detestation. To Boswell's smiling query, 'My dear Sir, you don't call Rousseau bad company. Do you really think *him* a bad man?' Johnson replied:

'Sir, if you are talking jestingly of this, I don't talk with you. If you mean to be serious, I think him one of the worst of men; a rascal, who ought to be hunted out of society, as he has been....Rousseau, Sir, is a very bad man. I would sooner sign a sentence for his transportation, than that of any felon who has gone from the Old Bailey

[1] *Life*, I, 448.   [2] *Works*, VI, 176.

these many years. Yes, I should like to have him work in the plantations.' BOSWELL. 'Sir, do you think him as bad a man as Voltaire?' JOHNSON. 'Why, Sir, it is difficult to settle the proportion of iniquity between them.'[1]

Yet his belief in the principle of subordination does not prevent his looking at the other side of the picture, as in an *Adventurer* (No. 111), where he writes:

I will confess, that I have sometimes employed my thoughts in examining the pretensions that are made to happiness, by the splendid and envied condition of life; and have not thought the hour unprofitably spent, when I have detected the imposture of counterfeit advantages, and found disquiet lurking under false appearances of gaiety and greatness.... What can any man infer in his own favour from a condition to which, however prosperous, he contributed nothing, and which the vilest and weakest of the species would have obtained by the same right, had he happened to be the son of the same father?[2]

If Johnson insisted on the necessity of deference to rank, he believed that a comparable obligation was owing on the other side. He was not at all uncertain how each should treat the other: 'I would behave to a nobleman as I should expect he would behave to me, were I a nobleman and he Sam. Johnson.' While he would 'no more deprive a nobleman of his respect than of his money', he expected equal consideration. Goldsmith having humorously complained that Lord Camden took no more notice of him 'than if I had been an ordinary man', and having raised a laugh at his own expense, Johnson, for the sake of friendship and the principle involved, ignored the jest: 'Nay, Gentlemen, (said he,) Dr Goldsmith is in the right. A nobleman ought to have made up to such a man as Goldsmith; and I think it is much against Lord Camden that he neglected him.'[3]

The classic example of such a meeting, where the due obligation was fulfilled on both sides, is of course John-

[1] *Life*, II, 11–12.   [2] *Works*, IV, 104, 108.
[3] *Life*, III, 311.

son's own interview with the King in the royal library—an interview from which both parties came away well pleased. 'Johnson talked to his Majesty', says Boswell, 'with profound respect, but still in his firm manly manner, with a sonorous voice.' And after the King withdrew, Johnson said, 'He is the finest gentleman I have ever seen'.[1] He told his friends later, 'I found his Majesty wished I should talk, and I made it my business to talk. I find it does a man good to be talked to by his Sovereign'.[2]

In spite of all this deference, he was extremely jealous of his independence, and careful never to give the least suggestion of personal subservience. 'No man', said he, 'who ever lived by literature, has lived more independently than I have done.'[3] The proud words are more than justifiable, even if the letter to Lord Chesterfield were not brought in evidence. He would write dedications to the whole Royal Family, to any of the nobility, for his friends, but he never penned a dedication in his own behalf. 'Such was his inflexible dignity of character', Boswell once wrote, 'that he could not stoop to court the great'; and he ended his life relatively poor, and little sought by titled visitors. Asked by Boswell, toward the close, whether he was discontented at having neither wealth nor place, he replied with a sturdy sense of reality:

'Sir, I have never complained of the world; nor do I think that I have reason to complain. It is rather to be wondered at that I have so much. My pension is more out of the usual course of things than any instance that I have known. Here, Sir, was a man avowedly no friend to Government at the time, who got a pension without asking for it. I never courted the great; they sent for me; but I think they now give me up. They are satisfied; they have seen enough of me.' Upon my observing [says Boswell], that I could not believe this,... he answered, 'No, Sir; great Lords and great Ladies don't love to have their mouths stopped.'... When I warmly declared how happy I was at all times to hear him;—'Yes, Sir, (said he); but if you were

[1] *Life*, ii, 40. [2] *Life*, ii, 42. [3] *Life*, i, 443.

Lord Chancellor, it would not be so: you would then consider your own dignity.'[1]

About the advantage of wealth Johnson was as realistic as he was unavaricious. When someone, in his presence, remarked that fortune and rank were nothing to a wise man, who would value only merit, Johnson overturned the airy theorist with practical wisdom:

'If man were a savage, living in the woods by himself, this might be true; but in civilized society we all depend upon each other, and our happiness is very much owing to the good opinion of mankind. Now, Sir, in civilized society, external advantages make us more respected. A man with a good coat upon his back meets with a better reception than he who has a bad one. Sir, you may analyse this, and say what is there in it? But that will avail you nothing, for it is a part of a general system...human felicity...is made up of many ingredients, each of which may be shewn to be very insignificant. In civilized society, personal merit will not serve you so much as money will. Sir, you may make the experiment. Go into the street, and give one man a lecture on morality, and another a shilling, and see which will respect you most. If you wish only to support nature, Sir William Petty fixes your allowance at three pounds a year; but as times are much altered, let us call it six pounds. This sum will fill your belly, shelter you from the weather, and even get you a strong lasting coat, supposing it to be made of good bull's hide. Now, Sir, all beyond this is artificial, and is desired in order to obtain a greater degree of respect from our fellow-creatures. And, Sir, if six hundred pounds a year procure a man more consequence, and, of course, more happiness than six pounds a year, the same proportion will hold as to six thousand, and so on as far as opulence can be carried. Perhaps he who has a large fortune may not be so happy as he who has a small one; but that must proceed from other causes than from his having the large fortune; for, *cæteris paribus*, he who is rich in a civilized society, must be happier than he who is poor; as riches, if properly used, (and it is a man's own fault if they are not,) must be productive of the highest advantages. Money, to be sure, of itself is of no use; for its only use is to part with it. Rousseau and all those who deal in paradoxes, are led away by a childish desire of novelty.'[2]

[1] *Life*, IV, 116.   [2] *Life*, I, 440–441.

In his *Journey to the Western Islands*, Johnson considers some aspects of the matter with greater formality. He adverts to the question of Highland justice, and reflects upon the relationship of wealth to power, in connection with the decline of feudalism among the Chieftains. 'No scheme of policy', he remarks,

has, in any country, yet brought the rich and poor on equal terms into courts of judicature. Perhaps experience, improving on experience, may in time effect it.

Those who have long enjoyed dignity and power, ought not to lose it without some equivalent.... When the power of birth and station ceases, no hope remains but from the prevalence of money. Power and wealth supply the place of each other. Power confers the ability of gratifying our desire without the consent of others. Wealth enables us to obtain the consent of others to our gratification. Power, simply considered, whatever it confers on one, must take from another. Wealth enables its owner to give to others, by taking only from himself. Power pleases the violent and proud: wealth delights the placid and the timorous. Youth therefore flies at power, and age grovels after riches.[1]

Poverty, Johnson came more and more to regard as an unmitigated ill. His letters to Boswell are full of exhortations to shun extravagance and live within his income.

Poverty, my dear friend, is so great an evil, and pregnant with so much temptation, and so much misery, that I cannot but earnestly enjoin you to avoid it. Live on what you have; live if you can on less; do not borrow either for vanity or pleasure; the vanity will end in shame, and the pleasure in regret.[2]

It is noteworthy that nine times out of ten his ground of abhorrence is not the immediate discomfort of personal deprivation, but rather the consequent inability of a poor man to relieve the miseries of others. Thus, he writes:

Poverty takes away so many means of doing good, and produces so much inability to resist evil, both natural and moral, that it is by all virtuous means to be avoided. Consider a man whose fortune is

[1] *Journey*, ed. Chapman, p. 85. [2] *Life*, IV, 149.

very narrow; whatever be his rank by birth, or whatever his reputation by intellectual excellence, what good can he do? or what evil can he prevent? That he cannot help the needy is evident; he has nothing to spare. But, perhaps, his advice or admonition may be useful. His poverty will destroy his influence: many more can find that he is poor, than that he is wise; and few will reverence the understanding that is of so little advantage to its owner. I say nothing of the personal wretchedness of a debtor, which, however, has passed into a proverb. Of riches, it is not necessary to write the praise. Let it, however, be remembered, that he who has money to spare, has it always in his power to benefit others; and of such power a good man must always be desirous.[1]

'A decent provision for the poor', Johnson once declared, 'is the true test of civilization.'[2] He himself never forgot the sufferings of the poor, never suffered others more fortunate to forget. 'He loved the poor', writes Mrs Thrale,

as I never yet saw any one else do, with an earnest desire to make them happy.—What signifies, says some one, giving halfpence to common beggars? they only lay it out in gin and tobacco. 'And why should they be denied such sweeteners of their existence (says Johnson)? it is surely very savage to refuse them every possible avenue to pleasure, reckoned too coarse for our own acceptance. Life is a pill which none of us can bear to swallow without gilding; yet for the poor we delight in stripping it still barer, and are not ashamed to shew even visible displeasure, if ever the bitter taste is taken from their mouths.'[3]

Two of the severest rebukes he ever administered to his beloved Mrs Thrale were for innocent remarks of hers which his own unsleeping preoccupation with misery turned to sudden illumination. Riding along in the parching summer heat, Mrs Thrale commenced to complain of the Surrey dust. Johnson was thundering at her in an instant: 'I cannot bear...when I know how many poor families will perish next winter for want of that bread which the present drought will deny them, to hear ladies

---

[1] *Life*, IV, 152. [2] *Life*, II, 130.
[3] *Johnsonian Miscellanies*, ed. Hill, I, 204–205 (Mrs Thrale's *Anecdotes*).

sighing for rain, only that their complexions may not suffer from the heat, or their clothes be incommoded by the dust;—for shame! leave off such foppish lamentations, and study to relieve those whose distresses are real!'[1] At another time, she was observing that she did not like goose because the smell of it, cooking, was so inescapable. Johnson said that this was the nicety of one who had never gone hungry, that to an unpampered appetite it was a delight to smell the dinner beforehand. Which pleasure, she replied, could be enjoyed in perfection by anyone who would pass through Porridge Island (a mean street full of cheap cookshops) in a morning. 'Come, come (says he gravely), let's have no sneering at what is so serious to so many: hundreds of your fellow-creatures, dear Lady, turn another way, that they may not be tempted by the luxuries of Porridge-Island to wish for gratifications they are not able to obtain: you are certainly not better than all of *them*: give God thanks that you are happier.'[2]

Nothing of this kind, however, surpasses Johnson's grave but shattering reproof of the facile optimism of Soame Jenyns, who, following Pope's arguments of the benefits of poverty, had the misfortune to pen the following remarks:

Poverty, or the want of riches, is generally compensated by having more hopes, and fewer fears, by a greater share of health, and a more exquisite relish of the smallest enjoyments, than those who possess them are usually blessed with. The want of taste and genius, with all the pleasures that arise from them, are commonly recompensed by a more useful kind of common sense, together with a wonderful delight, as well as success, in the busy pursuits of a scrambling world. ...Ignorance, or the want of knowledge and literature, the appointed lot of all born to poverty and the drudgeries of life, is the only opiate capable of infusing that insensibility, which can enable them to endure the miseries of the one, and the fatigues of the other.

[1] *Johnsonian Miscellanies*, ed. Hill, I, 218–219 (Mrs Thrale's *Anecdotes*).
[2] *Ibid.* I, 217–218.

It is a cordial, administered by the gracious hand of providence, of which they ought never to be deprived by an ill-judged and improper education. It is the basis of all subordination, the support of society, and the privilege of individuals; and I have ever thought it a most remarkable instance of the divine wisdom, that, whereas in all animals, whose individuals rise little above the rest of their species, knowledge is instinctive; in man, whose individuals are so widely different, it is acquired by education; by which means the prince and the labourer, the philosopher and the peasant, are, in some measure, fitted for their respective situations.[1]

Thus Soame Jenyns rests from God's labours, looks out upon the world, and behold! it is very good. He, too, is a great believer in subordination, and would not lay a finger on any part of the whole, lest he derange a system of which every minutest part fits exquisitely into its place.

To all such ineffable fatuity Johnson opposes his strong sense of actuality. He touches Jenyns's ideas and the sea-change they suffer is from pearls to rotting eyes, from coral to decaying bones:

Poverty is very gently paraphrased by want of riches. In that sense, almost every man may, in his own opinion, be poor. But there is another poverty, which is want of competence of all that can soften the miseries of life, of all that can diversify attention, or delight imagination. There is yet another poverty, which is want of necessaries, a species of poverty which no care of the publick, no charity of particulars, can preserve many from feeling openly, and many secretly.

That hope and fear are inseparably, or very frequently, connected with poverty and riches, my surveys of life have not informed me. The milder degrees of poverty are, sometimes, supported by hope; but the more severe often sink down in motionless despondence. Life must be seen, before it can be known. This author and Pope, perhaps, never saw the miseries which they imagine thus easy to be borne. The poor, indeed, are insensible of many little vexations, which sometimes imbitter the possessions, and pollute the enjoyments, of the rich. They are not pained by casual incivility, or mortified by the mutilation of a compliment; but this happiness is

[1] *A Free Inquiry into the Nature and Origin of Evil*, 1757, Letter II. The passage was dropped from later editions. It is quoted in Johnson's *Works*, VI, 53–54.

like that of a malefactor, who ceases to feel the cords that bind him, when the pincers are tearing his flesh. . . .

Concerning the portion of ignorance necessary to make the condition of the lower classes of mankind safe to the publick, and tolerable to themselves, both morals and policy exact a nicer inquiry than will be very soon or very easily made. . . . The bulk of mankind is not likely to be very wise or very good; and I know not, whether there are not many states of life, in which all knowledge, less than the highest wisdom, will produce discontent and danger. I believe it may be sometimes found, that a *little learning* is, to a poor man, a *dangerous thing*. But such is the condition of humanity, that we easily see, or quickly feel the wrong, but cannot always distinguish the right. Whatever knowledge is superfluous, in irremediable poverty, is hurtful, but the difficulty is to determine when poverty is irremediable, and at what point superfluity begins. Gross ignorance every man has found equally dangerous with perverted knowledge. . . .

Though it should be granted, that those who are *born to poverty and drudgery*, should not be *deprived*, by an *improper education*, of the *opiate* of *ignorance*; even this concession will not be of much use to direct our practice, unless it be determined, who are those that are *born to poverty*. To entail irreversible poverty upon generation after generation, only because the ancestor happened to be poor, is, in itself, cruel, if not unjust, and is wholly contrary to the maxims of a commercial nation, which always suppose and promote a rotation of property, and offer every individual a chance of mending his condition by his diligence. Those, who communicate literature to the son of a poor man consider him, as one not born to poverty, but to the necessity of deriving a better fortune from himself. In this attempt, as in others, many fail and many succeed. Those that fail, will feel their misery more acutely; but since poverty is now confessed to be such a calamity, as cannot be borne without the opiate of insensibility, I hope the happiness of those whom education enables to escape from it, may turn the balance against that exacerbation which the others suffer.

I am always afraid of determining on the side of envy or cruelty. The privileges of education may, sometimes, be improperly bestowed, but I shall always fear to withhold them, lest I should be yielding to the suggestions of pride, while I persuade myself that I am following the maxims of policy; and, under the appearance of salutary restraints, should be indulging the lust of dominion, and that malevolence which delights in seeing others depressed.[1]

[1] *Works*, VI, 54–57.

Consideration of poverty and its ills leads naturally to the larger question of which it is a part, the problem of evil. Jenyns's book as a whole was devoted to this problem: *A Free Inquiry into the Nature and Origin of Evil*. His solution is based on the old idea of a scale of being, to which Pope had given recent artistic expression in the *Essay on Man*. He posits a perfect universe, created and controlled by a perfect divinity: all evil, though undeniable in the parts, is good in relation to the whole. This system Johnson explodes as an absurd hypothesis, without taking any special credit for destroying a structure 'which is so ready to fall to pieces of itself'. The net result of Jenyns's inquiry, he declares at the end of his review, is that

after having clambered, with great labour, from one step of argumentation to another, instead of rising into the light of knowledge, we are devolved back into dark ignorance; and all our effort ends in belief, that for the evils of life there is some good reason, and in confession, that the reason cannot be found.[1]

What roused his ire was not the attempt itself, nor the inevitable failure, but the complacent spinning of metaphysical cobwebs as a coat of armour against the slings and arrows of outrageous fortune. 'The shame is', he insists, 'to impose words for ideas, upon ourselves or others. To imagine, that we are going forward, when we are only turning round. To think, that there is any difference between him that gives no reason, and him that gives a reason, which, by his own confession, cannot be conceived.'[2]

For one particular hypothesis of Jenyns he reserves his strongest, most ironic contempt. It is the notion that the universal system is so connected that the pain of one part of it benefits another part or parts, or even that there may be beings above us in the scale of creation, 'who may deceive, torment, or destroy us, for the ends, only, of their

[1] *Works*, vi, 75.   [2] *Works*, vi, 64.

own pleasure or utility', a hypothesis, according to Jenyns, impossible to conceive, but not the more improbable, and strongly confirmed by analogy.

I cannot [writes Johnson] resist the temptation of contemplating this analogy, which, I think, he might have carried further, very much to the advantage of his argument. He might have shown, that these 'hunters, whose game is man', have many sports analogous to our own. As we drown whelps and kittens, they amuse themselves, now and then, with sinking a ship, and stand round the fields of Blenheim, or the walls of Prague, as we encircle a cockpit. As we shoot a bird flying, they take a man in the midst of his business or pleasure, and knock him down with an apoplexy. Some of them, perhaps, are virtuosi, and delight in the operations of an asthma, as a human philosopher in the effects of the air-pump. To swell a man with a tympany is as good sport as to blow a frog. Many a merry bout have these frolick beings at the vicissitudes of an ague, and good sport it is to see a man tumble with an epilepsy, and revive and tumble again, and all this he knows not why. As they are wiser and more powerful than we, they have more exquisite diversions; for we have no way of procuring any sport so brisk and so lasting, as the paroxysms of the gout and stone, which, undoubtedly, must make high mirth, especially if the play be a little diversified with the blunders and puzzles of the blind and deaf. We know not how far their sphere of observation may extend. Perhaps, now and then, a merry being may place himself in such a situation, as to enjoy, at once, all the varieties of an epidemical disease, or amuse his leisure with the tossings and contortions of every possible pain, exhibited together.

One sport the merry malice of these beings has found means of enjoying, to which we have nothing equal or similar. They now and then catch a mortal, proud of his parts, and flattered either by the submission of those who court his kindness, or the notice of those who suffer him to court theirs. A head, thus prepared for the reception of false opinions, and the projection of vain designs, they easily fill with idle notions, till, in time, they make their plaything an author; their first diversion commonly begins with an ode or an epistle, then rises, perhaps, to a political irony, and is, at last, brought to its height, by a treatise of philosophy. Then begins the poor animal to entangle himself in sophisms, and flounder in absurdity, to talk confidently of the scale of being, and to give solutions which himself confesses impossible to be understood. Sometimes, however, it happens, that their pleasure is without much mischief. The author feels no pain, but while they are wondering at the extravagance of his opinion, and pointing him out to one another, as a new example of human folly, he is enjoying his own applause and that of his companions, and, perhaps, is elevated with the hope of standing at the head of a new sect.

Many of the books which now crowd the world, may be justly suspected to be written for the sake of some invisible order of beings, for surely they are of no use to any of the corporeal inhabitants of the world.... The only end of writing is to enable the readers better to enjoy life, or better to endure it; and how will either of those be put more in our power, by him who tells us, that we are puppets, of which some creature, not much wiser than ourselves, manages the wires! That a set of beings, unseen and unheard, are hovering about us, trying experiments upon our sensibility, putting us in agonies, to see our limbs quiver; torturing us to madness, that they may laugh at our vagaries; sometimes obstructing the bile, that they may see how a man looks, when he is yellow; sometimes breaking a traveller's bones, to try how he will get home; sometimes wasting a man to a skeleton, and sometimes killing him fat, for the greater elegance of his hide.

This is an account of natural evil, which though, like the rest, not quite new, is very entertaining, though I know not how much it may contribute to patience. The only reason why we should contemplate evil is, that we may bear it better; and I am afraid nothing is much more placidly endured, for the sake of making others sport.[1]

Johnson himself has nothing to offer in place of Jenyns's fantastic notions. The problem is too vast, too appalling, too important for him to do more than confess his ignorance. Like Browning's Grammarian, he refused to discount life, to 'draw a circle premature':

> He ventured neck or nothing—heaven's success
> Found, or earth's failure.

There is a paper in *The Idler* which puts in outline form but with admirable clarity the position which Johnson believed man without presumption could adopt toward evil. It is, of course, not in the least unorthodox, but it is useful to-day to be reminded of the precise boundaries of

[1] *Works*, VI, 64–66.

orthodoxy. Johnson starts by asserting that philosophy is unequal to the task of accounting for the origins of evil. He then states without comment the religious explanation of its involvement with sin; but proceeds at once to demonstrate that most of the moral good to be discovered in the world is the direct consequence of physical evil. Taking the convenient theological classifications, he divides goodness into soberness, righteousness, and godliness. 'Sobriety, or temperance, is nothing but the forbearance of pleasure; and if pleasure was not followed by pain, who would forbear it?' Righteousness, or the system of social duty, consists of justice and charity, both of which obviously rise from the same source. The inconveniences of injustice drive men to submit to restraint; and charity could not be practised were there no want. Of godliness, or piety, he declares:

None would have recourse to an invisible power, but that all other subjects have eluded their hopes. None would fix their attention upon the future, but that they are discontented with the present. If the senses were feasted with perpetual pleasure, they would always keep the mind in subjection. Reason has no authority over us, but by its power to warn us against evil.[1]

The religious training of our earliest years is soon crowded out by the immediate concerns of life, and only 'some pressing and resistless evil'—illness, decay, the death of those from whom we derive our pleasures—brings us back at last to the shelter of religion:

That misery does not make all virtuous, experience too certainly informs us; but it is no less certain that of what virtue there is, misery produces far the greater part. Physical evil may be, therefore, endured with patience, since it is the cause of moral good; and patience itself is one virtue by which we are prepared for that state in which evil shall be no more.[2]

[1] *Idler*, No. 89, December 29, 1759. *Works*, IV, 413.
[2] *Works*, IV, 414.

If the range and character of Johnson's thinking have been at all fairly represented in the foregoing cento of quotations, we are justified in describing this mind as one which perceived with sufficient acuteness the fundamental contradictions between logic and life, but which, though driven by its own strength toward the attempt, refrained at all the ultimate gates from forcing a passage to synthesis. The curb which held him back is perfectly distinct, and his yielding to its pressure quite deliberate. His dislike of the metaphysicians does not arise from a rationalizing of his own intellectual inferiority. He believed that the farthest one could go in philosophy was not far enough to penetrate ultimate obscurities or make any practical difference to humanity. Metaphysical systems existed in a vacuum; while the tremendous mysteries of life and death beat, every hour, inexorably at man's door. The first could be put aside; the latter could not be ignored. What, therefore, could make one give oneself to the former except intellectual vanity or a childish love of novelty?

Hume, and other sceptical innovators, are vain men, and will gratify themselves at any expence.... If I could have allowed myself to gratify my vanity at the expence of truth, what fame might I have acquired. Every thing which Hume has advanced against Christianity had passed through my mind long before he wrote. Always remember this, that after a system is well settled upon positive evidence, a few partial objections ought not to shake it. The human mind is so limited, that it cannot take in all the parts of a subject, so that there may be objections raised against any thing. There are objections against a *plenum*, and objections against a *vacuum*; yet one of them must certainly be true.[1]

And again:

Human experience, which is constantly contradicting theory, is the great test of truth. A system, built upon the discoveries of a great many minds, is always of more strength, than what is produced by the mere workings of any one mind, which, of itself, can do little. ...As to the Christian religion, Sir, besides the strong evidence

[1] *Life*, I, 444.

which we have for it, there is a balance in its favour from the number of great men who have been convinced of its truth, after a serious consideration of the question.[1]

It is hard to believe, in the face of his intellectual habit and what he says about reasons, that Johnson was naturally religious, or that it would not have been much easier, temperamentally, for him to have been a sceptic. His violence about it is the measure of the desperate fight which it cost him to hold fast his religion. The mind that is predisposed to religion feels itself adrift until it comes to anchor in the harbour of a firm and happy faith. Johnson's mind was of the opposite variety: it was most congenially occupied in inquiry. He was not made happy by taking things on faith; and *credo quia impossibile est* antagonized his strongest instincts. It is a question whether his religion did not bring him more continuous disquiet than it ever brought comfort, till the very end. Once, when he had run across a sermon of Blair's which he much admired, he qualified his praise thus: 'There is one part of it which I disapprove...which is, that "he who does not feel joy in religion is far from the kingdom of heaven!" There are many good men whose fear of God predominates over their love. It may discourage. It was rashly said.'[2] Certainly religion was not a mild and sunny element in his life, but crossed with storm and struggle. The very reasons he gives for religious belief are rooted in distress and misery, and they come from him without qualification or mitigation, as we have seen: 'None would have recourse to an invisible power, but that all other subjects have eluded their hopes.' Little of joyous acceptance here! Religion is a *pis aller* to which one is driven by the desperate character of the quest for happiness.

---

[1] *Life*, I, 454.

[2] *Life*, III, 339. I note with interest a somewhat similar point of view with regard to Johnson's religion in a recent book, *The Forgotten Hume*, by Ernest C. Mossner, New York, 1943, pp. 204–207.

More than once Johnson described the world as a place in which we can find 'absolute misery, but happiness only comparative: we may incur as much pain as we can possibly endure, though we can never obtain as much happiness as we might possibly enjoy'.[1] The same sentiment informs his greatest poem and its prose counterpart:

> Yet hope not life from grief or danger free,
> Nor think the doom of man revers'd for thee.

In this state, where pain so predominates over pleasure, where reason so often falters, and where even the best of men may be working irreparable harm when they think to do good, religious revelation confers upon us the benefit of an invariable rule 'by which we may be certain to promote the general felicity, and be set free from the dangerous temptation of *doing evil that good may come*'. Because it

may easily happen, and, in effect, will happen, very frequently, that our own private happiness may be promoted by an act injurious to others, when yet no man can be obliged, by nature, to prefer, ultimately, the happiness of others to his own; therefore, to the instructions of infinite wisdom, it was necessary that infinite power should add penal sanctions. That every man, to whom those instructions shall be imparted, may know, that he can never, ultimately, injure himself by benefiting others, or, ultimately, by injuring others benefit himself; but that, however the lot of the good and bad may be huddled together in the seeming confusion of our present state, the time shall undoubtedly come, when the most virtuous will be most happy.[2]

III. 'RECAPITULATION'

It is of the essence of Johnson's nature that his very acceptances should be strenuous, hard won and with difficulty held. 'To strive with difficulties', he once wrote, 'and to conquer them, is the highest human felicity; the

---

[1] *The Adventurer*, No. 111. *Works*, IV, 105.
[2] *Works*, VI, 71–72.

next is, to strive, and deserve to conquer: but he whose
life has passed without a contest, and who can boast
neither success nor merit, can survey himself only as a
useless filler of existence; and if he is content with his own
character, must owe his satisfaction to insensibility.'[1] It
is the ideal of a born fighter; and it is another of the
apparent contradictions in him that Johnson always spoke
of war in terms of abhorrence, instead of being driven to
become its apologist. 'Well', he once said after a lively
dinner party, 'we had good talk.' 'Yes, Sir', said his com-
panion sardonically, 'you tossed and gored several persons.'[2]

We have seen Johnson as a young man attacking
established positions, taking the 'wrong side' of every
question, flying at the eagle. We have seen him, through
half his life, the vigorous opponent of the government.
We have also seen him, especially in the latter years of his
life, stoutly conservative, if not reactionary, in his defence
of an undemocratic House of Commons, and with regard
to taxing the American colonies. It would be a great mistake to join with the detractors who accused him of
venality upon receiving his pension; but it would be
almost as wrong to think of him as a man who swung from
revolutionary sentiments to arch-conservatism as his blood
cooled with age. There is, in fact, very little of the cooling
process to be seen. His habit of mind remains aggressive,
his style of expression athletic, up to the end. The greater
ease is no slackening of vigour: increased suppleness and
elasticity are not a sign of hardening of the arteries. What
happens to Johnson's prose is analogous to the transformation of iron to steel, instead of to the setting in of
crystallization. 'I will be conquered; I will not capitulate',
was said in the last months of mortal existence.

There is something radically wrong, therefore, about

[1] *The Adventurer*, No. 111. *Works*, iv, 108.
[2] *Life*, ii, 66.

the conventional habit of thinking of him, historically, as a glacial deposit, indicative of the limits of an expended force. The image obscures the dynamic quality of his whole life—of his later years equally with his earlier. Seen truly, the conservatism of the last two decades is marked by a resistance to dominant forces which is little different, at bottom, from that of the young iconoclast. The change which he appears to have undergone is in reality rather outside him than within. The general current of thought is now flowing strongly in the opposite direction. Hume and Voltaire and Rousseau supply momentum, and are joined by the multitude of tributaries, the freethinkers and levellers, who all sweep giddily toward the cascade of the 'nineties. To talk the new doctrines was not to be merely fashionable, but to be in harmony with the deepest temper of the time. In opposing them, Johnson was not practising simple passive resistance, but putting forth more vigorous effort than he had ever had to exert in his youth. Temperamentally, then, he is always in revolt; and the conservatism of his maturity only *appears* to be a denial of his natural instincts.

Conservative and *radical* mean different things at different times. That which was once conservative may, when new ground has been won, assert itself to a later generation as radical. It would take us too far beyond the scope and centre of the present study of a man to consider properly the significance of these conflicting political and social philosophies to our own time. But it may be allowable to say that a society based upon the acceptance of the dogmas of *laissez-faire* can hardly regard Johnson's theory of the necessity of subordination as a very conservative doctrine. Read in other terms, it is obviously closer to socialistic thought than it is to the premises of modern capitalism. A society reluctantly coming to acknowledge the necessity of drastic modification in the system of free competition will look with different eyes upon a theory which takes that necessity for granted to such an extent that Whiggism, the political expression of capitalistic tenets, is considered 'the negation of all principle'. If conservatism aims at maintaining the *status quo*, and progressivism at such change as may promote the better satisfaction of the ends of social organization, Johnson, as a convinced opponent of the present *status quo*, would range himself to-day on the side of progressivism. This is not to justify his political philosophy, nor need we waste time in idle speculation as to his hypothetical position. It is enough that he condemned wholeheartedly the theoretical bases of a system which is now everywhere giving ground.

There is, in fact, scarcely a finer example of the Johnsonian irony in all his works than that which disposes of the *laissez-faire* ideal, in its Rousseauan guise, in the twenty-second chapter of *Rasselas*. The philosopher who puts the ideal has expressed great impatience with hopes of distant happiness, and maintains that happiness is within all men's grasp:

'The way to be happy is to live according to nature, in obedience to that universal and unalterable law with which every heart is originally impressed; which is...not instilled by education, but infused at our nativity.... Other men may amuse themselves with subtle definitions, or intricate ratiocinations. Let them learn to be wise by easier means: let them observe the hind of the forest, and the linnet of the grove; let them consider the life of animals, whose motions are regulated by instinct: they obey their guide, and are happy. Let us therefore, at length, cease to dispute, and learn to live; throw away the encumbrance of precepts,...and carry with us this simple and intelligible maxim,—that deviation from nature is deviation from happiness.'

When he had spoken, he looked round him with a placid air, and enjoyed the consciousness of his own beneficence. 'Sir', said [Prince Rasselas] with great modesty, 'as I, like all the rest of mankind, am desirous of felicity, my closest attention has been fixed upon your discourse; I doubt not the truth of a position which a man so learned has so confidently advanced:—let me only know what it is to live according to nature.'

'When I find young men so humble and so docile', said the philosopher, 'I can deny them no information which my studies have enabled me to afford.—To live according to nature, is to act always with due regard to the fitness arising from the relations and qualities of causes and effects; to concur with the great and unchangeable scheme of universal felicity; to co-operate with the general disposition and tendency of the present system of things.'

The prince soon found that this was one of the sages whom he should understand less as he heard him longer. He therefore bowed and was silent; and the philosopher, supposing him satisfied, and the rest vanquished, rose up, and departed with the air of a man that had co-operated with the present system.

How radically opposed Johnson is to allowing men to consult their free inclinations on the ground that, so, the best interests of society would ultimately be served, is again illustrated in the argument upon Vicious Intromission. Human life, he declares,

from a degree of savageness and independence, in which all laws are vain, passes or may pass, by innumerable gradations, to a state of reciprocal benignity, in which laws shall be no longer necessary. Men are first wild and unsocial, living each man to himself, taking from the weak, and losing to the strong. In their first coalitions of society, much of this original savageness is retained. Of general happiness, the product of general confidence, there is yet no thought. Men continue to prosecute their own advantages by the nearest way; and the utmost severity of the civil law is necessary to restrain individuals from plundering each other. The restraints then necessary, are restraints from plunder, from acts of publick violence, and undisguised oppression. The ferocity of our ancestors, as of all other nations, produced not fraud, but rapine. . . . As manners grow more polished, with the knowledge of good, men attain likewise dexterity in evil. Open rapine becomes less frequent, and violence gives way to cunning. Those who before invaded pastures and stormed houses, now begin to enrich themselves by unequal contracts and fraudulent intromissions. . . . I am afraid the increase of commerce, and the incessant struggle for riches which commerce excites, gives us no prospect of an end speedily to be expected of artifice and fraud.[1]

[1] *Life*, ii, 198.

There are, then, two insuperable objections to the Rousseauan thesis and all the talk about Nature's Simple Plan. The first is, that there is no such plan save in the pages of vain innovators; and the second, that to restore the state of nature is to bring back the reign of Chaos and Old Night.

But the nature of Johnson's conservatism may be tried in another, less theoretical, way. We may ask whether, in the face of ameliorable ills and iniquities of his time, Johnson resisted improvement, and for what reasons. In such an inquiry we ought to distinguish between general cases and cases involving individuals, for a man often excepts his friends from their kind.

Of his unwillingness to leave unrighted any individual wrong that came to his attention, or individual suffering unalleviated, there need be no long question. Boswell is full of illustrations of his active benevolence, and everyone knows of it. He made his home a hospital; he emptied his pockets for others; he begged, which is harder; he pleaded by letter and by word of mouth; and the evidence in Boswell, undoubtedly, covers not a tithe of the good he did. It was not merely for personal friends. He pleaded the case of Admiral Byng in the public prints, believing, and truly, that Byng was being made the scapegoat of governmental ineptitude. Johnson had almost no personal acquaintance with Dr Dodd; yet he wrote paper after paper on behalf of this convicted forger, pleading for leniency, offering spiritual consolation, and in fact living through his suffering with him. Charity hospitals, causes like the clothing of French prisoners of war, found in him, as we have seen, an active friend. He was kind to the downtrodden and the outcast; he gave shelter to prostitutes, relieved the distress of debtors, gave all his silver to beggars. He wrote letters of consolation to the bereaved; he befriended authors with practical assistance, revising their manuscripts, writing dedications, and winning patrons for them.

But again, of general social wrong, where it did not challenge the principle of subordination, he was equally ready to work for improvement. He opposed the use of the press gang for recruiting the Navy. He hated the institution of slavery with all the force of his nature. Among a company of grave Oxford dons, his toast was, 'Here's to the next insurrection of the negroes in the West Indies.'[1] It is curious to hear him appealing to nature as an argument against the slave trade:

It may be doubted [he declares], whether slavery can ever be supposed the natural condition of man. It is impossible not to conceive that men in their original state were equal; and very difficult to imagine how one would be subjected to another but by violent compulsion....A man may accept life from a conquering enemy on condition of perpetual servitude; but it is very doubtful whether he can entail that servitude on his descendants; for no man can stipulate without commission for another....The rights of nature must be some way forfeited before they can be justly taken away.[2]

There is an argument made to the hand of Rousseau and the American colonists!

Again and again Johnson recurs to the evil of imprisonment for debt and the ills that follow in its wake. He contributed three papers to *The Adventurer* on the subject; and two more, in *The Idler*,[3] are very powerful pleas for a change in the law. Innocent, he says, or merely improvident, or even benevolent, beings are thrown among the most depraved of mankind and at the same time deprived of every means of rescuing themselves from these surroundings, and languish till death or 'till malevolence shall relent'. He estimates that five thousand persons

[1] *Life*, III, 200.
[2] *Life*, III, 202–203.
[3] *Adventurer*, Nos. 41, 53, 62; *Idler*, Nos. 22, 38.

48

perish in debtors' prisons every year, 'overborne with sorrow, consumed with famine, or putrefied with filth', and declares passionately:

The misery of gaols is not half their evil: they are filled with every corruption which poverty and wickedness can generate between them; with all the shameless and profligate enormities that can be produced by the impudence of ignominy, the rage of want, and the malignity of despair...if there be any reason why this inveterate evil should not be removed in our age, which true policy has enlightened beyond any former time, let those, whose writings form the opinions and the practices of their contemporaries, endeavour to transfer the reproach of such imprisonment from the debtor to the creditor, till universal infamy shall pursue the wretch whose wantonness of power, or revenge of disappointment, condemns another to torture and to ruin; till he shall be hunted through the world as an enemy to man, and find in riches no shelter from contempt.

Surely, he whose debtor has perished in prison, although he may acquit himself of deliberate murder, must at least have his mind clouded with discontent, when he considers how much another has suffered from him; when he thinks on the wife bewailing her husband, or the children begging the bread which their father would have earned. If there are any made so obdurate by avarice or cruelty, as to revolve these consequences without dread or pity, I must leave them to be awakened by some other power, for I write only to human beings.[1]

The severity of the laws with regard to felonies was another evil which exercised Johnson's humane concern. From medieval times, as new conditions had arisen, new offences had seemed to deserve the most drastic treatment, until in 1770 Blackstone estimated the number of capital crimes at one hundred and sixty at the least. None had been expunged, though values in property and in money had changed enormously. The consequent absurdities and barbarities in the penal code are beyond the powers of imagination to conceive. To pick a man's pocket of more than a shilling, for example, or to make it possible for fish to escape from a fishpond, were crimes punishable by

[1] *Idler*, No. 38. *Works*, IV, 262–263.

death; but attempted murder, perjury leading to an innocent man's death, arson under conditions endangering the lives of multitudes, were not capital offences. To steal two pounds' worth of goods from a river boat was capital; but not to steal the same amount on a canal: for when the law had been made there had been no canals, and no one now wished to impose the death penalty for so small a crime.[1]

On the abuse of the death penalty, Johnson wrote a finely reasonable paper for *The Rambler* (No. 114), showing how the very frequency and caprice of its occurrence kept it from being an effective deterrent. So many disproportions, he declared, between crimes and punishments, such capricious distinctions of guilt, such confusions of remissness and severity, are no evidence of public wisdom:

> To equal robbery with murder is to reduce murder to robbery; to confound in common minds the gradations of iniquity, and incite the commission of a greater crime to prevent the detection of a less. If only murder were punished with death, very few robbers would stain their hands in blood; but when, by the last act of cruelty, no new danger is incurred, and greater security may be obtained, upon what principle shall we bid them forbear?...
>
> The frequency of capital punishments, therefore, rarely hinders the commission of a crime, but naturally and commonly prevents its detection, and is, if we proceed only upon prudential principles, chiefly for that reason to be avoided. Whatever may be urged by casuists or politicians, the greater part of mankind, as they can never think that to pick the pocket and to pierce the heart is equally criminal, will scarcely believe that two malefactors so different in guilt can be justly doomed to the same punishment: nor is the necessity of submitting the conscience to human laws so plainly evinced, so clearly stated, or so generally allowed, but that the pious, the tender, and the just, will always scruple to concur with the community in an act which their private judgment cannot approve....
>
> The obligations to assist the exercise of publick justice are indeed strong; but they will certainly be overpowered by tenderness for life. What is punished with severity contrary to our ideas of adequate retribution, will be seldom discovered; and multitudes will be

[1] Cf. Lecky, *England in the Eighteenth Century*, VI, 245 ff.

suffered to advance from crime to crime, till they deserve death, because, if they had been sooner prosecuted, they would have suffered death before they deserved it.[1]

Yet, in spite of this wise and humane attitude, Johnson could complain, when the iniquitous procession of the condemned from Newgate to Tyburn was at last abolished —could lament that Tyburn itself was not free from the fury of innovation that was driving the age mad! Executions, he roundly declared, failed of their intended effect if there was no public procession to impress the imagination and 'support the criminal'. He must have known—Richardson, forty years earlier, had described their debauchery[2]—that these spectacles were nothing more than riotous and sadistic holidays to the London mob. Even so, and with all necessary subtractions, it is impossible, in the face of the foregoing record, to think of Johnson as in any just sense a 'reactionary'.

IV. 'CODA'

It was said at the start that Johnson's most characteristic utterance, and the turbulent imagination and impulsive temperament of the man, belonged to a poet. If the feelings of the reader have at all corresponded with those of the transcriber of his sentiments, this assertion has meanwhile crystallized into conviction. In the deepest sense of the word—in his imaginative apprehension of the quality and texture of experience, in his dynamic attitude to life and its values, in his need of the shaping expression of his perceptions—he was a poet, a *maker*.

There is a memorable passage by another combative spirit which, theology apart, epitomizes that attitude of tragic optimism which was Johnson's very being—the sombre conviction, together with the radical, even physio-

---

[1] *Rambler*, No. 114. *Works*, III, 41–43.
[2] Cf. *Familiar Letters upon Important Occasions*, No. CLX.

logical, affirmation of his nature. The words are familiar, but their present application reinforces our understanding:

> I confess that I do not see why the very existence of an invisible world may not in part depend on the personal response which any one of us may make to the religious appeal. God himself, in short, may draw vital strength and increase of very being from our fidelity. For my own part, I do not know what the sweat and blood and tragedy of this life mean, if they mean anything short of this. If this life be not a real fight, in which something is eternally gained for the universe by success, it is no better than a game of private theatricals from which one may withdraw at will. But it *feels* like a real fight,—as if there were something really wild in the universe which we, with all our idealities and faithfulnesses, are needed to redeem; and first of all to redeem our own hearts from atheisms and fears. For such a half-wild half-saved universe our nature is adapted....
>
> These then are my last words to you: Be not afraid of life. Believe that life *is* worth living, and your belief will help create the fact. The 'scientific' proof that you are right may not be clear before the day of judgment....But the faithful fighters of this hour...may then turn to the faint-hearted, who here decline to go on, with words like those with which Henry IV greeted the tardy Crillon after a great victory had been gained: 'Hang yourself, brave Crillon! We fought at Arques, and you were not there!'[1]

There, likewise, is Johnson's deepest response to existence. Not with the bounding optimism of Rabbi Ben Ezra, yet with instinctive satisfaction of imperious inner compulsions, he grappled with a world in which joy was three parts pain, grimly but somehow exultantly fighting the good fight, determined never to capitulate.

[1] William James, *The Will to Believe and Other Essays*, 1927 ed., pp. 61–62.

BOSWELL'S BOSWELL

James Boswell never got used to the fact that his father did not think so well of him as he himself did. 'He is a man of sense', James once wrote to his friend Temple, 'and a man of worth. But from some unhappy turn in his disposition, he is much dissatisfied with a son whom you know.'[1] There is much in this disharmony to engage our interest and divide our sympathies. Alexander Boswell, Lord Auchinleck, the biographer's father, possessed in ample measure the typical virtues of the Scottish character: he was prudent, inflexible of principle, sturdily self-reliant, a man who kept to his course though the heavens should fall. His son, on the contrary, had none of the conventional virtues, though many of the vices, of his race: he was of an outgoing disposition, mercurial, an inveterate gossip, overfond of drink, deplorably lax in sexual conduct, inexhaustibly prolific of hare-brained projects, as undependable as the weather of his native hills. But it is to this son's genius—a genius compounded inextricably of his volatile with his solider qualities—that posterity owes such a debt of gratitude as not many men in the world's history can claim; while the only claim of the father upon our remembrance is his involuntary gift of the son he would have preferred to suppress, and from whom he actually did extract a written renunciation of his birthright.

'I write to him with warmth, . . . wishing that he should think of me as I am; but my letters shock him',[2] Boswell complained. But had Alexander Boswell lived to the age of Methuselah, growing in wisdom the while, he could

[1] *Letters of James Boswell*, ed. C. B. Tinker, Oxford, 1924, i, 127.
[2] *Loc. cit.*

not have succeeded in thinking of James as he was. And it may well be doubted whether anyone else, from his day to ours, has plucked out the heart of that mystery. For Boswell is a complex and baffling personality. Boswell's personal papers, lately recovered, have provided fuller evidence for the study of his inner private history than perhaps exists for any other human being of whom we have record. What may not be generally realized is that these revelations have increased instead of lessening the difficulty of comprehending truly this extraordinary being. Had Boswell been invented by a novelist, we should at once reject the character as an amiable monster, credible only at rare moments. Faced with the incontrovertible evidence of his actual, daily existence as he wrote it down, with appalling frankness, for his own private perusal, there is still the strongest temptation, after an initial effort to make something convincing out of it in terms of human character, to give over the attempt and gaze unbelieving at the fantastic spectacle. And in this bewilderment we should very often have the company of Boswell himself. 'My life', he wrote to Temple, in a letter which oscillates in three pages through all the 360 degrees, 'is one of the most romantic that I believe either you or I really know of; and yet I am a very sensible, good sort of man. What is the meaning of this, Temple?'[1]

The nineteenth century was pretty generally agreed about the meaning of it, and was satisfied to know no more of him than was forced on the attention by his published works. Macaulay stated the position with finality in a famous and paradoxical paragraph:

That he was a coxcomb and a bore, weak, vain, pushing, curious, garrulous, was obvious to all who were acquainted with him. That he could not reason, that he had no wit, no humour, no eloquence, is apparent from his writings. And yet his writings are read beyond

[1] *Letters*, I, 108.

the Mississippi, and under the Southern Cross, and are likely to be read as long as the English exists, either as a living or as a dead language. Nature had made him a slave and an idolater. His mind resembled those creepers which the botanists call parasites, and which can subsist only by clinging round the stems and imbibing the juices of stronger plants. He must have fastened himself on somebody.... In a happy hour he fastened himself on Johnson.... During twenty years the disciple continued to worship the master: the master continued to scold the disciple, to sneer at him, and to love him.... Boswell... could pay only occasional visits to London. During those visits his chief business was to watch Johnson, to discover all Johnson's habits, to turn the conversation to subjects about which Johnson was likely to say something remarkable, and to fill quarto note-books with minutes of what Johnson had said. In this way were gathered the materials, out of which was afterwards constructed the most interesting biographical work in the world.[1]

It is this paragraph, so full of contradictions—containing enough truth to explode its own mischievous perversions on a thoughtful reading, and enough plausible misrepresentation to obliterate the truth which it holds,—that the unthinking world has chosen to adopt as Boswell's veritable image. There have been protests and there have been attempts, latterly more frequent, to substitute a closer likeness for Macaulay's cheap chromo. But, one after the other, they go down like ninepins before Boswell's own records. The worst have been the thumbnail sketches, like Lytton Strachey's, which have tried to seize the essentials of his character in a memorable aphorism: 'Boswell was *ex hypothesi* absurd: it was his absurdity that was the essential condition of his consummate art.'[2] This does not even rise to Macaulay's level. The best and truest approaches have been those of Sir Walter Raleigh and Professor Chauncey Tinker, and, more recently, of Geoffrey Scott and Professor F. A. Pottle, who accept the factor of genius as a cardinal consideration for analysis, and refuse to

[1] Macaulay's *Life of Johnson*, first published in the *Encyclopædia Britannica*, 1856.

[2] Lytton Strachey, *Portraits in Miniature*, New York, 1931, p. 90.

sit in judgment upon the man. Led by Professor Tinker, most recent students of Boswell have tried harder to understand than to arraign him. But his latest full-length biographer is an exception who deserves a special word.

C. E. Vulliamy, in *James Boswell*, 1933, has painted the cruellest and most damaging portrait of his subject that has ever been composed. Drawing on the new stores of information, he claims authority and affects impartiality. In the interests of truth, he will not minimize Boswell's absurdities, nor sprinkle rose water over the discreditable passages of his life. 'The aim of biography', he nobly declares, 'should be to avoid taking sides, and to present... the true history of action, thought and circumstance....'¹ With unflagging vivacity, and with the journalist's eye for arresting detail and picturesque episode, Vulliamy traces Boswell's earthly career, inventing nothing, omitting little that may add piquancy to the story. His comments, however, fall short of his lofty objective. It is difficult to discover any impartiality, harder still to detect any sympathy, in his book. Boswell, we are told, in his private journals, and in his babbling letters to Temple, 'has prepared, for the peering psychologist, a garbage-pie of the most extraordinary dimensions.... Had this exposure of himself been the instrument of a personal reformation, or even made with a sincere moral purpose, it would have been less objectionable. True, there are crises of remorse and vows of repentance; and then the story goes on again, with cackles of stupid laughter and all the sorry antics of a disordered vanity'.² Even in the mere narrative, the judge everywhere seizes the pen and expresses his sense of outrage. When chapter follows chapter in this indignant tone, the naïve reader is ready to suppose that the author despises his man. But no! there is a surprise in store for us, a secret

¹ C. E. Vulliamy, *James Boswell*, New York, 1933, p. viii.
² *Ibid.* p. 58.

that has been saved, not without hints of something in reserve, till the end of the book. After a devastating reconsideration of Macaulay's opinion, in which all the contemptuous epithets are approved and reinforced, we learn at last that Boswell is not to be blamed, because the man was, quite literally, mad: 'it was congenital insanity that drove him to drink and every wild indulgence; and those indulgences at last destroyed him. The biographical data cannot lead to any other conclusion'.[1] After two hundred and fifty pages of vigorous denigration, the book closes on the note of pity. We ordinary, normal persons 'will not be ashamed of trying to think kindly of Boswell and of pointing to the better side of his unfortunate disposition'; and, in view of the 'comfort, relief, and delight' which his work has brought to 'innumerable thousands', 'mere gratitude, mere decency will make us compassionate'.[2] It remains but to say that any hint of that desiderated compassion, as well as any analysis of the talent which composed the *Life of Johnson*, is to seek between the covers of this volume.

To turn a biography into a mystery story is, I think most readers will agree, not the way to arrive at a wise understanding of character. 'Did these bones cost no more the breeding than to play at loggats with 'em?' If Boswell was congenitally insane, it would have been useful to know it sooner. The contempt poured upon the doomed wretch now seems a little irrelevant: we might have saved much virtuous indignation for a more appropriate occasion.

Perhaps Boswell *was* mad. For that matter, perhaps also Hamlet was mad. Until our analyses of insanity grow more precise, however, we shall do well to reserve the term for more positive cases. In the present state of

[1] C. E. Vulliamy, *James Boswell*, New York, 1933, p. 269.
[2] *Ibid.* p. 270.

our knowledge, there is more to be gained by trying to understand Boswell than by clapping a label on him which would preclude the attention of anyone but a psychiatrist. Oddity his vast circle of friends and acquaintances was ready enough to allow him; but if every Briton who strikes others as odd is, by the same token, to be dubbed insane, let us all put in at once for the post of Gravedigger at Elsinore.

It is probable that there are multitudes of human beings who pass with more or less credit through the world who, if they recorded all their thoughts and acts with a Pepysian frankness, would expose themselves to a pelting from the midden of unsavoury epithet. Believing this, one may not consistently visit upon Boswell a contempt which is not equally deserved by the rest of the world. Where others have been silent, Boswell has been vocal. In fairness, one should limit one's special blame of Boswell to the charge of folly in writing down for his own view what other men prefer to ignore or to conceal even from themselves. But if this be the nature of the charge against him, it becomes at once clear that *folly* may be the wrong word. The saint, the moralist, the scientist, and the artist can all provide grounds in view of which it may appear not merely blameless, but even wise and meritorious to follow such a course. Nevertheless, the ninety and nine will continue to vilify the one who exposes himself for whatever reason; and, if his outward conduct have left much to be desired, no apology will serve. There are very few of us who, reading the record of Boswell's existence, cannot often, on one count or another, flatter ourselves with superiority to him. The chief danger, therefore, which the would-be biographer of Boswell must guard against is this of condescension. Where condescension enters, Boswell's natural proportions shrink, his genius escapes, and we are left with nothing but a caricature. In truth, Boswell demands of us

—or rather, takes for granted—the last degree of forbearance and patient sympathy; but only by meeting these requirements can we even begin to understand him. This is not an idle caveat: it is certain that before his self-analysis has been followed even for a tenth of its total extent, Boswell will have alienated a great part of his audience.

It requires no prolonged search among his letters and journals to find passages which may serve as touchstones of our moral and intellectual tolerance and of the measure of our imaginative sympathy. The brevity of the following extract recommends it to the purpose:

Saturday 21 *December* [1765].
. . . I recalled my charming Signora at Sienna, and was disgusted at all women but her, and angry at myself for being in the arms of another. Susette chatted neatly and diverted me. I sacrific'd to the graces. I think I did no harm.

Sunday 22 *December.*
I found I was now above being taken in by Whores. I viewed with pity the irregularitys of humanity. I went to hear mass; but was too late. . . . I went . . . to visit Mr Grenville, who was stately but affable. He pleased me. I have attained such a happy frame of mind that envy never disturbs me, and I can calmly admire a man of merit just as I admire a fine picture. It is merit which engages me, be it in myself or in others.*

If, upon reading the foregoing passage, the chief ingredient of our laughter is found to be scorn, whether for the morals, or for the simplicity, or for the vanity of Boswell, we may be sure we are not in a condition to form a just image of the man. We may then either try to alter

---

* All quotations in this essay from Boswell's Journals are from the *Private Papers of James Boswell from Malahide Castle*, originally published in a limited edition by William Rudge (18 vols.; New York, 1928-1934). An unlimited edition under the editorship of Professor Frederick A. Pottle has been published by the McGraw-Hill Book Company and William Heinemann, Ltd. Grateful acknowledgment for permission to quote is hereby accorded to Yale University, the McGraw-Hill Book Company, and Messrs. Heinemann. For the present extract, cf. *Private Papers*, VII, 41.

our attitude or turn elsewhere, for the strain of long keeping company with him will otherwise prove too great.

II

In perusing Boswell's journals, one is struck by the lack of solidity and permanence in his idea of himself. The image in his mind is as if drawn in smoke. The lightest breath will obliterate its outlines, and when the pattern again takes shape, it is not the same. To be sure, he cannot picture himself as other than a notable figure, but what particular role to settle upon in the pursuit of fame he has no idea. The multiplicity of his potentialities bewilders him. Apparently, habit has no significance: he never speaks of it, never seems to realize it as a conditioning factor in his existence. Like Bottom the weaver, Boswell finds nothing of which he is aware in human emotion or experience really alien to his disposition. He 'likes whate'er he looks on, and his looks go everywhere'. The parallel is entirely unforced:

BOTTOM. Let me play the lion too.... I will roar, that I will make the duke say 'Let him roar again, let him roar again.'

BOSWELL. One evening,...when Dr Hugh Blair and I were sitting together in the pit of Drury-lane play-house, in a wild freak of youthful extravagance, I entertained the audience *prodigiously*, by imitating the lowing of a cow.... I was so successful in this boyish frolick, that the universal cry of the galleries was, '*Encore* the cow! *Encore* the cow!' In the pride of my heart [he adds], I attempted imitations of some other animals, but with very inferior effect.[1]

Habitually, he sees himself momentarily as different persons of his acquaintance whom, for one quality or another, he admires. He often sets down in his diary his feeling that on a particular occasion he was 'quite' his father or some other personal friend. Or he will counsel

[1] Boswell's *Journal of a Tour to the Hebrides*, ed. R. W. Chapman, Oxford, 1930, p. 428.

himself to 'be' one of his acquaintances. In this imaginative identification with others, Boswell went far beyond mere metaphor. The histrionic element in him was as abnormally strong as his sense of his own identity was abnormally indistinct. His quick sensibility, perceptive eye, and prodigious memory registered the impress of other personalities with waxlike fidelity. That he was a wonderful mimic could almost have been assumed. But his own consciousness of this talent is admirable. In conversation with Rousseau, he declares that, though he has now given it up, he used to be a perfect virtuoso in mimicry, collecting personalities like a connoisseur. Turning back to a convivial evening in 1762, we find him recording his immediate sense of this virtuosity: 'I was all spirit and entertained them prodigiously. I began this night to take off Mr David Hume which I did amazingly well. Indeed it was not an imitation but the very Man. I had not only his external address, but his sentiments and mode of expression.'[1] Boswell was then twenty-two years old; Hume was fifty and famous.

But we are not restricted to his own testimony. Fanny Burney, who loved and admired Dr Johnson and was by no means partial to Boswell, admitted that Boswell's imitation of the Doctor's manner was not caricature at all: 'indeed,' she writes on one occasion, 'his imitations, though comic to excess, were so far from caricature that he omitted a thousand gesticulations which I distinctly remember.'[2] Again, Hannah More recalls having been umpire in a contest between Boswell and David Garrick, to see which could best imitate Johnson's manner: she gave her verdict for Garrick in reciting poetry, but for Boswell in familiar conversation.[3] When one remembers

[1] *Private Papers*, I, 135. (See footnote on p. 59, above.)
[2] *Diary and Letters of Madame D'Arblay*, ed. Austin Dobson, 1904, V, 83.
[3] *Johnsonian Miscellanies*, ed. G. B. Hill, 1897, II, 195.

that the greatest actor of his age had known Johnson intimately since boyhood, and that Boswell did not meet Johnson until the latter was past fifty, nor keep company with him thereafter for a full year of days altogether, one asks no further evidence of Boswell's talent.

The value of such a gift to the biographer of Johnson is apparent when we think of Boswell's method of recording conversation. No other talent could so well have assisted a phenomenal memory in re-creating dialogue from abbreviated memoranda. It served Boswell as an instrument by which, having fixed the sentiments and the key words, he was able to test the turns of phrase and the cadences of Johnson's speech to see that, as reconstructed, they rang true. The boast which we discount with laughter in connection with Hume, we are forced to accept *au pied de la lettre* when translated into the solidity of the Johnsonian record.

The recurrent declarations in his journals that he was 'quite' somebody of his acquaintance are Boswell's recognition of the fact that at a certain moment his floating emotions and impressions of himself had crystallized into a definable shape. But more often it was not so. What he had to register as the very stock-in-trade of his journalizing was the discordant and gusty waywardness of his emotional attitudes from hour to hour and from day to day. He was endlessly fascinated by the mere discontinuity of his orientations toward experience, and regarded the record of these changes as one of the most important features of his self-imposed task.

Any consecutive series of extracts would exhibit this preoccupation. Consider, for example, the sequence of entries as he left Holland and commenced a tour through the petty states and courts of Germany in the summer of 1764. He starts off 'in a charming frame, quite blissful', with his blood circulating briskly. He is a new man, with new ideas and 'no gloomy fears'. On the 28th of June he goes to bed in such 'vast spirits' that he cannot sleep. Next day he has 'fallen not a little'. On the 30th he has sunk into melancholy. 'My thoughts were horrid; yet my manners were chearfull.' On the 1st of July he is moderately recovered. By the 2nd he feels like a Don Quixote, rising on the 3rd to great and pleasing thoughts. He tumbles again on the 4th into gloom, and cannot 'relish this rich scene as Boswell himself relishes Beauty'. The foul fiend flies on the 5th, and the 6th finds him 'firm and gay and sound as ever'. On the 7th he feels himself just the figure of a young Scottish laird, but he sinks again next day. By the 10th his new lodgings, with a 'genteel, large Alcove' and a 'pretty silk bed', bring with them a new accession of happiness, convincing him of the necessity for him of the 'small elegancies' of life; and on the 13th he rises 'fresh as a Roe on the Braes of Lochaber'.[1] So one might go on, week after week, fascinated like him with this emotional kaleidoscope; but it is already clear that Sterne was not the only Englishman who made a Sentimental Journey across the Continent in this decade of the 1760's.

III

Boswell's habit in keeping his journals was to make an abbreviated memorandum of the events of the day, either before going to bed or next morning; and to follow this at leisure by a fuller account in regular diary form. Enough of the original memoranda have survived to reveal an interesting fact. In them, Boswell habitually addresses himself in the second person. Probably most people do this when making notes of things yet to be done. But surely few practise the form except in the imperative, and fewer

---

[1] *Private Papers*, III, 10 ff.

still when referring to the past. Boswell constantly writes to himself in this style. '[You] received a letter from Mr. Johnson treating you with esteem and kindness', he will record: '[you were] nobly elated by it, and resolved to maintain the dignity of yourself.'[1]

Now this use of the second person is a highly indicative trait in Boswell. It calls attention to his double consciousness of himself. This state of mind in him deserves our close observation. With the keenest awareness of immediate sensations, he displays at the same time an even stronger impulse toward the objective view. The divided vision is constant to him. Frequently the cleavage is so wide that the two rôles seem independent of each other, simultaneously activated by different intelligences. The split between actor and spectator appears strikingly in a passage in which he describes a heated argument with his father on a question which mattered tremendously to him. In the midst of the dispute, he is suddenly moved to urge reasons which strike him at the time as so extraordinary that he can barely keep a straight face while he utters them; yet all the while he is in the utmost anxiety to convince his opponent.

Of the two halves of his consciousness, the observer's, one comes to believe, is the deeper and more vital half. The doer moves with almost automatic response through a giddy flux of involuntary event and emotion; but the intelligence that sits apart and ponders the spectacle is a comparatively steady reality. Here, in truth, is the explanation of Boswell's journals. It is in response to the deepest need of his being that he keeps this record. In a very real sense the journals, as Geoffrey Scott has observed, *are Boswell's life*; his actual daily existence was not. His mere existence was the literal exemplification of Hume's discontinuous present; but the consciousness that registered

1 *Private Papers*, VII, 60.

it and brooded over it, and tried to puzzle out of it a rational pattern and a definable purpose, was a continuous identity. A conversation at the Thrales', recorded in the *Life of Johnson*, hints at Boswell's own sense of the fact. 'As a lady', he there remarks, 'adjusts her dress before a mirror, a man adjusts his character by looking at his journal.'[1]

There can be little doubt that this detachment of Boswell the observer from Boswell the actor had much to do with the naked frankness of the record, and with its fullness. The actor appeared to the observer so singular, so unexpected and changeable, so foreign, that one could never safely leave anything to inference, or to the laws of cause and effect. One could not reconstruct such an existence by a set of principles, presumptively; one could only follow it *a tergo*, with unremitting attention, careful to trace every slightest movement on to the page. Moreover, one need not be too much dismayed by the odd and disreputable conduct of such a being: one could at any rate do nothing about it at the time, one could not tax oneself with responsibility for these vagaries, which one had neither foreseen nor yet professed to understand. One need not therefore be troubled unduly by a sense of personal shame, nor refrain from putting down what actually happened. Besides, it must be admitted that the creature under observation *was* fascinating. Because of this psychological distancing, Boswell found it possible, one cannot but believe, to be both more brutally candid in registering discreditable facts and more flatteringly indulgent in reporting creditable ones.

Boswell's habitual mental state has close analogies with the child's faculty of make-believe. Absorbed in his game, the child can tell himself to 'be' any person or thing, and for him it is so. But all the time he remains himself, his

[1] Boswell's *Life of Johnson*, ed. G. B. Hill and L. F. Powell, Oxford, 1934, III, 228.

divided consciousness poised above the real and ideal states of being. If the child could actually externalize his make-believe, he would be a Boswell. For Boswell is like a child who, in a never-never-land, has, to his delighted amazement, seen his make-believe self suddenly projected into a solid physical reality, from which he knows his real self distinct, though inseparable. So long as the spell remains, he can neither wholly resume his own identity nor completely identify himself with the figure he sees.

If this description be too fanciful, we can find a more familiar analogy in the dream state. The kind of awareness that is manifest in Boswell's attitude is an extension of the psychology of the ordinary dreamer. Like the latter, Boswell goes through a series of situations, preternaturally aware of what is happening, but somehow curiously detached, irresponsible, a mere interested onlooker. His existence is an odd inversion of ordinary life. The waking state has, as it were, become the dream state. The reality of his own everyday life is more phantasmagorical and less solid to him than the imaginary world of a dream.

As frequently with the dreamer, Boswell is always confident that he is almost at the point of awaking out of this present unreality into reality. He assures himself time after time that the moment is approaching when he will be himself: 'You may depend upon it', he writes to Temple, 'that very soon my follies will be at an end, and I shall turn out an admirable member of society.'[1] At times he feels able to name the very minute of awakening. One of the times when he felt surest that the hour was about to strike was just before the publication of his first important book. Temple, as usual, was the recipient of his confidence.

Temple, I wish to be at last an uniform pretty man. I am astonishingly so already; but I wish to be a man who deserves Miss

[1] *Letters*, I, 108.

B[lair, the goddess of the moment]. . . I am always for fixing some period for my perfection as far as possible. Let it be when my *Account of Corsica* is published. I shall then have a character which I must support. I will swear like an ancient disciple of Pythagoras to observe silence; I will be grave and reserved, though chearful and communicative of what is *verum atque decens*.[1]

In anticipation of the day, he tidied up accounts, and paid all his visits outstanding, intending thenceforward, as he said, 'to maintain a propriety and strictness of manners'.[2]

For a time Boswell was actually under the illusion that the awakening had occurred. Conscious of his own importance, he felt a kind of sober elevation in company; and, as soon as he could get free from legal duties, he set off for London, in order to savour to the full his newly acquired character. He travelled down with gay companions and felt an agreeable sense of superiority when he saw them making thoughtlessly merry:

I was now become quite composed, and never spoke for speaking's sake, or was uneasy because I was silent. The truth is I am now conscious of having attained to a superiour character, and so rest satisfied. . . . After my former sufferings from bad health and low spirits, I exulted in my present vigour and chearfullness. . . . I thought of marriage and was determined to have a good match, as I was become so agreable and so happy a man.[3]

In this excellent frame he reaches London. He and his friends enjoy a good meal together and he goes off to his lodgings in Piccadilly. 'After unpacking my trunk', he writes (the entry is of the same date as the last), 'I sallied forth like a roaring Lion after girls, blending philosophy and raking.' The busy day is concluded with his going to the Consul's, where he sups and is 'quite hearty'. The next three days pass in much the same excitement, and then he coaches down to Oxford to see Johnson. He spends three sober days in Johnson's company, and gathers a

[1] *Letters*, I, 137.   [2] *Private Papers*, VII, 144.
[3] *Ibid*. VII, 162.

budget of admirable conversation which later was to find a place in the *Life*. He returns to London and resumes his sportive existence just where he left off. For a considerable part of the following month he is, by a natural consequence, confined to his chambers; but his discomfort is alleviated by the visits of a large number of distinguished men, the names of many of whom are still familiar to us. At this point, he writes as follows to his confessor:

My dear Temple,

Your moral lecture came to me yesterday, in very good time, while I lay suffering severely for immorality. If there is any firmness at all in me, be assured that I shall never again behave in a manner so unworthy the friend of Paoli. My warm imagination looks forward with great complacency on the sobriety, the healthfulness, and the worth of my future life.[1]

The rest of the letter is filled with the merits of Zélide, a well-born and brilliant Dutch lady, who had just written him after several years' silence a letter to which he had immediately replied with an offer of marriage, declaring, 'I am now I think a very agreable man to those who know my merit and excuse my faults'.[2]

Boswell had been sadly mistaken in thinking that his salad days were over. And he continued to make the same mistake almost to the end of his life. The truth is, his character never 'jelled'. His marriage to Margaret Montgomerie—a woman of real nobility of character—gave him temporary stability; and from time to time his career was less vertiginous than usual. But for the most part, as Geoffrey Scott felicitously observes, Boswell 'kept his good resolutions by writing them down and redressed his back-sliding by copying them out'. The last decade of his existence, which produced the *Life of Johnson*, produced in addition as many rash enterprises and vain expectations as any other part of his career.

[1] *Letters*, I, 153.　　　　　[2] *Private Papers*, II, 71.

IV

The adolescent attitude he never really outgrew. Yet no man ever watched with more pathetic eagerness for signs that the period of probation was over; no man ever felt a keener desire for improvement or a sharper need to be a person of steady consequence and solid worth. His radical uncertainty of his own identity made it enormously important to him to possess the respect and esteem of others.

It is impossible to doubt that the desire for self-betterment was one of the deepest roots of the luxuriant growth of self-analysis that fills volume after volume of his private journals. One hears the ground-bass of this longing beneath every one of the never-ending series of variations that he continues to improvise while life endures. In some of the passages already cited the theme has been audible; but it is worth pausing over one or two of his more pronounced efforts to improve.

At Utrecht, after a prolonged period of despondency, he collected his energies and drew up an impressive document entitled 'Inviolable Plan', which he undertook to read over at the commencement of each day. In it he reminded himself of his promising potentialities, of the expectations of his relatives and friends. By study and diligence, he noted, he had already acquired a firmness which he was now to consolidate by filling his mind with worthy objects, with thoughts of religion, morality, and the dignity of human nature. Recommending to himself a philosophical persistence, he concludes with happy auguries of being an excellent character and of gaining the approbation of the world. The general doctrine of the 'Plan' was supplemented from time to time with special notes of advice for particular occasions.[1]

[1] Cf. e.g. *Private Papers*, ii, 185 ff.

One of his most considerable efforts toward self-improvement was a series of periodical essays which in middle age he engaged to write at regular intervals and which appeared each month for almost six years in the pages of *The London Magazine*, under the title of *The Hypochondriack* (admirably edited in 1928 by Margery Bailey). By these essays, which are not devoid of intrinsic merit, he hoped to prove to himself—for he kept the secret of their authorship from all but a very few friends—that he had the steadiness to discharge a recurrent duty, as well as the requisite knowledge and ability to maintain the interest and value of such a performance.

It is probable that Boswell's persistent desire for self-improvement could be traced to the effect upon him in boyhood of his father's influence and example. Of his relationship to his mother not much is to be learned: he associates with her memory a simple and trusting piety. But evidence of the impact of his father's personality upon him is continuous and abundant. The relationship need not here be analysed in detail: the main lines of it are clear. Lord Auchinleck very early discerned his son's quickness of parts and made it plain that what was expected—nay, required—of such promising abilities was a nearly perfect performance. Pressure was applied in various ways. We learn that one of Lord Auchinleck's devices was to give his son a 'premium' for every ode of Horace he memorized: James dutifully got by heart more than forty—and to the end of his life could quote an apt Horatian phrase when the need arose. When the boy tried hard to live up to expectations, the father was pleased and indulgent. But the stern judge had absolutely no sympathy for childish fallibility, nor any tolerance for indecision or infirmity of purpose. With his father in mind, Boswell was later to write in one of the 'Hypochondriacks':

Young men, though keen and impetuous, are usually very well disposed to receive the counsels of the old, if they are treated with gentleness, and as their minds are not as yet taught distrust by repeated disappointment, or fretted by painful incidents, they give large credit for wisdom to those who have lived longer than themselves. But old men forget in a wonderful degree, their own feelings in the early part of life, are angry because the young are not as sedate in the season of effervescence as they are, would have the fruit, when by the course of nature there should be only the blossom, and complain because another generation has not been able to ascend the steep of prudence in the fourth part of the time which they themselves have taken.[1]

His father's expectations were an Atlas's load for James, who was anxious to excel, sensitive to parental displeasure, and quite intelligent enough to see how intimately the universal esteem in which his father was held was connected with the latter's possession of those qualities and acquirements which were now recommended to his own practice.

Lord Auchinleck, himself strong-willed, could naturally see no pressing need to develop determination in another member of his family: he expected entire submission to his judgment and conformity to his desires. Yet he expected also that, where it did not conflict with his own will, James's steadiness of purpose should be equally strong. In consequence, the son's genius was rebuked under the father to such a degree that James never ceased to feel like a child in his father's presence. Boswell's essay on Parents and Children (*Hypochondriack*, June, 1781) contains, under cover of anonymity, a most revealing piece of autobiography:

If young men be accustomed to the most abject dependence on unlimited authority in an individual, it would seem their spirits must be broke, so as that they never can attain to that manly resolution without which we never enjoy liberty...we see fathers who very injudiciously, and in my opinion very unjustly, attempt to keep

[1] *The Hypochondriack*, ed. Margery Bailey, 1928, I, 169.

their sons even when well advanced in life, in such a state of subjection as must either reduce them to unfeeling stupidity, or keep
them in perpetual uneasiness and vexation. At what period parental
power of compulsion should cease, and be succeeded by voluntary
filial reverence, cannot be exactly ascertained....One thing however is certainly right—that the change should be gradual, that a
son may imperceptibly arrive at the dignity of personal independence, so as not to be intoxicated and abuse it. If a father has not
consideration enough to keep this in view, and accommodate himself accordingly, he will lose in a great measure the satisfaction and
comfort of having a son. I knew a father who was a violent whig,
and used to attack his son for being a tory, upbraiding him with
being deficient in 'noble sentiments of liberty', while at the same
time he made this son live under his roof in such bondage, that he
was not only afraid to stir from home without leave like a child,
but durst scarcely open his mouth in his father's presence. This was
sad living.[1]

A striking entry in his journal, written three years earlier
than the foregoing, describes how once, on the point of
setting off for London, Boswell would take leave of his
father only in the presence of his own little daughter: his
intention was to circumvent his usual depressing timorous-
ness in the old man's presence, by reminding himself that
he too was a parent, and not a mere child. It was, he says,
like having a little footstool to increase his stature.[2] His
father, he complained over and over again, could not bear
that his son should talk with him as a man.

Yet Lord Auchinleck was never absolutely unreasonable, never gratuitously unkind. Boswell acknowledges
recent favours of a very substantial kind in the same letters
in which he complains of his treatment. If his father had
been more inhuman, it would probably have been well for
James; for an actual breach that could be justified to
himself on any solid grounds might have forced Boswell
early to develop his own principles. As it was, he could
neither live according to his father's standards nor ration-

[1] *The Hypochondriack*, ed. Margery Bailey, 1928, ii, 89ff.
[2] *Private Papers*, xiii, 103.

72

ally reject them. He had nothing to substitute that seemed to him half so good. A touching instance of his admiration appears in an earlier part of his diary. Passing through Lyons in 1766, he looked on the city, he remarks, with a degree of reverence because of an idea that his father had once spent some time there.[1] The parent continued to hold his son's respectful admiration as in a vice, and never quite lost his affection, in spite of almost continual and most mutual exasperation. More than once, in his letters to Temple, he expresses his keen regret at being denied the 'pious satisfaction' of being on good terms with his father. 'How hard', he exclaims, 'is it that I am totally excluded from parental comfort.'[2] Once he dreamed that his father had died. He awoke in tears, and resolved anxiously to be more subservient to his parent's wishes, so as to have nothing to regret in later years. But when, next morning, he saw his father in the flesh, the latter's cold indifference froze his tender sentiments.[3]

So, by Lord Auchinleck's dominance, the twig had been bent; and Boswell was conditioned from the start to look outside himself for guidance. The record of his friendships is the record of a long series of attempts to substitute a more congenial mentor and model for the rigid figure of his father. David Hume, Lord Kames, Dr Blair, Lord Marischal, Sir John Pringle, Voltaire, Rousseau, General Paoli, Dr Johnson: every one of the men to whom he attached himself and in whose company he most delighted was a man of his father's generation, distinguished for some excellence, whether of character, influence, or intellect. All his closest friendships, with the solitary exception of that with Temple, subsisted on the unequal basis of pupil and master—and Temple was a clergyman, and therefore had an equivalent title to

[1] Cf. *Private Papers*, VII, 55.   [2] *Letters*, I, 235.
[3] Cf. *Private Papers*, XI, 90.

authority. 'Admonish me,' he begs of Temple, 'but forgive me.'[1] In his journal, Boswell once wrote, apropos a remark of Johnson's:

> I really feel myself happier in the company of those of whom I stand in awe than in any other company....[It] composes the uneasy tumult of my spirits, and gives me the pleasure of contemplating something at least comparatively great.[2]

When he first sought out Johnson, he was twenty-two and Johnson fifty-four—almost exactly his father's age. The world called him a tuft-hunter. Doubtless, that element was not lacking in his egoistic disposition. But far more fundamental was the almost pathetic hunger of his nature for firm leadership, the need to sit at the feet of authority, to have the weight of his doubts and fears and uncertainties lifted from him, if only for a time. Even his relationship with his wife—the one permanent friendship he ever had with a member of the opposite sex—shows a strong tincture of the filial. 'I am fully sensible', he writes to Temple,

> ...of my happiness in being married to so excellent a woman, so sensible a mistress of a family, so agreable a companion, so affectionate and peculiarly proper [a] help-mate for me. I own I am not so much on my guard against fits of passion or gloom as I ought to be; but that is really owing to her great goodness. There is something childish in it, I confess. I ought not to indulge in such fits; it is like a child that lets itself fall purposely, to have the pleasure of being tenderly raised up again, by those who are fond of it.[3]

In Johnson, more completely than in any other being he ever met, Boswell found the sustenance his nature craved. Here was strength of character, here was abundance of knowledge, here was God's plenty of precept and example, here was wisdom welling, in phrases of superb eloquence, out of a mind of startling individuality and power, out of a heart widely and deeply acquainted with

[1] *Letters*, I, 102.   [2] *Private Papers*, XIII, 41.
[3] *Letters*, I, 180.

74

human life. It was as little of an accident as such a thing
could be that Boswell found Johnson out. He had already
been stirred by Johnson's writings, and came up to
London determined to meet him. And when he did meet
him, he refused to be put off by a rebuff which for most
people would have precluded all further acquaintance,
because he knew at once (and it is an honour to him), he
knew in his innermost being, what he had found. What
Johnson, in turn, saw in Boswell, after a preliminary meeting or two, was a being whose human need for just what
he had to give was very nearly desperate. There is never
any question, in the mind of either, of equal status in their
friendship, or on what basis it is founded. Boswell was
not pushing himself into Johnson's society for any un-
justifiable reason. Describing in the *Life* their fourth
meeting—an unplanned one,—Boswell records his motives
with simple candour:

Finding him in a placid humour, and wishing to avail myself
of the opportunity which I fortunately had of consulting a sage, to
hear whose wisdom I conceived...that men filled with a noble
enthusiasm for intellectual improvement would gladly have resorted
from distant lands;—I opened my mind to him ingenuously, and
gave him a little sketch of my life, to which he was pleased to listen
with great attention.... Being at all times a curious examiner of
the human mind, and pleased with an undisguised display of what
had passed in it, he called to me with warmth, 'Give me your hand;
I have taken a liking to you.'[1]

Inside of a mere two months we find Johnson travelling
all the way to Harwich to see Boswell off for the Continent. Considering the discrepancy of their minds and
ages, the spectacle on intellectual grounds is absurd. On
grounds of humanity, considering Boswell's need and
Johnson's active benevolence and awareness of that need,
nothing could be more natural and appropriate.

[1] *Life*, I, 404–405.

75

Boswell had found the one in whose strength and wisdom his weakness and his ignorance could place a perfect reliance. In Johnson's presence he becomes the sort of person he wishes at his best moments to be; and that is why, off in Germany, the mere thought of Johnson uplifts him.[1] Johnson is already the polestar of his existence; and he feels that if he can have the assurance of the great man's perpetual friendship, it will be a certain support throughout his life. Lying stretched upon the tomb of Melanchthon, with romantic solemnity he writes to Johnson, vowing an eternal attachment; and nearly at the same time declares, in a letter to Lord Kames, that he regards his friendship with Johnson as the happiest event of his life, and boasts of the honour of his correspondence. 'The Conversation of that great and good man', he writes, 'has formed me to manly Virtue, and kindled in my mind a generous ardour which I trust shall never be extinguished.'[2] Boswell had at this date received but one letter from Johnson; but he was right in calling it an honour, for it was the magnificent long letter of needful advice which he later printed in the *Life* (*sub* 1763): 'Resolve, and keep your resolution: choose, and pursue your choice.'[3]

This, then, is the basis of that memorable friendship; and it is odd to reflect that if Boswell had been better adjusted, or merely on harmonious terms with his father, there would have been no *Life of Johnson* to delight the world. For in a real sense—though the statement must not stand as a sufficient explanation of that book—the *Life* is the almost involuntary tribute of a great human weakness to a great human strength. It was in the first instance his own need that caused Boswell to put forth the enormous effort of remembering what Johnson said in his

[1] Cf. *Private Papers*, III, 49. [2] *Ibid.* III, 102.
[3] *Life*, I, 475.

presence and afterward to go to the labour of setting it down. Not unjustifiably he writes in his Advertisement to the first edition of the *Life*: 'The stretch of mind and prompt assiduity by which so many conversations were preserved, I myself, at some distance of time, contemplate with wonder.'[1] It must not be thought that Boswell ran about ·the world like an animated dictograph, recording whatever conversation came within earshot. It is a testimony to his superb recording that so many scenes in the *Life* are living drama; but originally there was only one voice which he was really concerned to record, and the rest is there to give occasion to that voice. We are, I think, likely to be misled by the convincing reality of Johnson's conversation into assuming that the conversation of others is equally true to life. True to life, in the sense of being uninvented and authentic as far as it goes, it certainly is; but Boswell himself would not have it supposed an adequate representation of his own or anyone else's conversational powers except Johnson's. What comes close enough to the Johnsonian core of light is caught and fixed; the rest dims out toward invisibility. To cite Boswell's own remarks, as reported in the *Life*, as evidence of the paucity of his ideas is therefore grossly unfair. What he tried to preserve in his journal was Johnson's *ipsissima verba*, primarily because of their value to him. But the very words of himself or of others were relatively unimportant. An unkind and exaggerated picture by Fanny Burney indicates Boswell's concentration in Johnson's presence:

The moment that voice burst forth, the attention which it excited in Mr Boswell amounted almost to pain. His eyes goggled with eagerness; he leant his ear almost on the shoulder of the Doctor; and his mouth dropt open to catch every syllable that might be uttered: nay, he seemed not only to dread losing a word, but to

---

[1] *Life*, I, 6.

be anxious not to miss a breathing; as if hoping from it, latently, or mystically, some information.[1]

v

Primarily, then, this 'stretch of mind and prompt assiduity' were exerted for his private benefit and instruction. But there was another impulse almost equally strong which drove him in the same direction. Boswell was so fascinated by the spectacle of life, he had such a zest and relish for it, that he was impelled to try to save as much of it as possible from oblivion. In an early journal he makes the curious and significant remark: 'I should live no more than I can record, as one should not have more corn growing than one can get in. There is a waste of good if it be not preserved.'[2]

Life at the workaday level, however, has few charms for so mercurial a temperament. His instinctive ideal is perfectly expressed in the Conclusion of Pater's *Renaissance*:

Not the fruit of experience, but experience itself, is the end. A counted number of pulses only is given to us of a variegated, dramatic life. How may we see in them all that is to be seen in them by the finest senses? How shall we pass most swiftly from point to point, and be present always at the focus where the greatest number of vital forces unite in their purest energy? To burn always with this hard, gemlike flame, to maintain this ecstasy, is success in life.[3]

But Boswell would hardly have agreed with Pater that the highest degree of this 'quickened, multiplied consciousness' was to be found in Art. And it is worth while to try to determine a little more exactly what the ingredients of the most vivid and valuable experience were for him, what qualities were requisite to this ideal intensity. With the help of his journals, we are able to make them out with

[1] *Memoirs of Dr Burney*. Quoted from C. B. Tinker, *Dr Johnson and Fanny Burney*, New York, 1911, p. 224.
[2] *Private Papers*, XI, 150.
[3] Pater's *The Renaissance*, ed. 1903, pp. 249–250.

a fair measure of accuracy. They appear to be three in number.

Ranging them in ascending order, the first essential is that the inner excitement shall be exactly commensurate with the external stimulus. This correspondence does not for Boswell have to be tested by any metaphysical considerations of the nature of reality—though upon rare occasions he may avail himself of such ideas as an excuse for indecision. Ordinarily, the outward world is as solid to him as it was to Dr Johnson's foot. He wishes to take the universe of phenomena at its face value, and is anxious not to discount it by some cloudiness of apprehension, some irrelevant distraction or depression of spirits, some mistiness on the pane of his perceptions:

I was drest the first time at Ferney [Voltaire's chateau] in my Seagreen and Silver, and now in my flowered velvet. Gloom got hold of me at dinner.... It hurt me to find that by low spirits it is possible for me to lose the relish of the most illustrious Genius. Hard indeed![1]

The second requirement is that his awareness of the special quality of the present moment of felicity shall be intensified by comparison and contrast with other scenes, and heightened by being looked at in as many lights as possible. Thus at a Court Ball in Germany:

I danced with her Royal Highness, who danced extremely well. We made a very fine english Minuet.... What a group of fine ideas had I! I was dancing with a Princess, with the Grand-daughter of King George whose Birth-day I have so often helped to celebrate at old Edinburgh, with the daughter of the Prince of Wales, who patronized Thomson and other votaries of Science and the Muse; with the Sister of George the Third, my Sovereign. I mark this variety, to show how my Imagination can enrich an Object; so that I have double pleasure when I am well. It was noble to be in such a frame.... I was next taken out to dance by the Princess Elizabeth, who is to be Queen of Prussia, and by the Princess Dorothea. My spirits bounded; yet was I solemn, and stretched my view to the world of futurity.[2]

[1] *Private Papers*, IV, 139, 137.   [2] *Ibid.* III, 56

While all melts under our feet [to quote Walter Pater again], we may well catch at any exquisite passion, or any contribution to knowledge that seems by a lifted horizon to set the spirit free for a moment, or any stirring of the senses, strange dyes, strange colours, and curious odours, or work of the artist's hands, or the face of one's friend. Not to discriminate every moment some passionate attitude ...is, on this short day of frost and sun, to sleep before evening. With this sense of the splendour of our experience and of its awful brevity, gathering all we are into one desperate effort to see and touch,...what we have to do is to be for ever curiously testing new opinions and courting new impressions, never acquiescing in a facile orthodoxy.[1]

Boswell's involuntary embodiment of this philosophy is surely startling. 'You have told me', he once wrote to Temple,

that I was the most *thinking* man you ever knew. It is certainly so as to my *own life*. I am continually *conscious*, continually *looking back* or *looking forward* and wondering how I shall feel in situations which I anticipate in fancy. My *journal* will afford materials for a very curious narrative. I assure you I do not now live with a view to have surprising incidents, though I own I am desireous that my life should *tell*. [By *tell* he probably means not *count*, but *recount*.][2]

This passage was written in 1789, when the flaming wick of his existence was nearly guttering in the socket.

However it might be by that time—and even here we must discount his sobriety, for in the very same letter he says his roving disposition may quite possibly one day carry him to Asia, and speaks of himself as 'full of ambition and projects to attain wealth and eminence',—so eager a curiosity, so passionate a zest for experience could never have permitted him to wait passively for what life might bring. He had always lived 'with a view to have surprising incidents', and it is this aggressive—or better, creative—side of his nature that provides the third element in his notion of high felicity.

The aspect of Boswell's character that led him toward adventure was compounded in about equal parts of

---

[1] Pater, *loc. cit.*   [2] *Letters*, II, 371–372.

scientific curiosity and romantic imagination. Endlessly curious as to how 'that animal called man' worked, he was impelled to probe the recesses, to explore the odd angles, of human nature. He was never happier than when, following up some obscure bypath or twisting lane, he had stumbled upon some unsuspected facet of character, or brought out a potentiality hitherto dormant. Forever on the prowl, his eager interest spared others no more than himself. His imagination was as inexhaustibly fertile in suggesting human experiments as his ingenuity was indefatigable in devising the machinery for carrying them out. The *Journal of a Tour to the Hebrides with Samuel Johnson, LL.D.* is the undying record of his greatest single experiment; but many of the most telling scenes in the *Life*, like the dinner at Dilly's, are equally vivid reports of smaller experiments, and the Journals contain the clinical record of scores of minor ones. For example, he visits a condemned man, his client, in his cell, two or three days before execution. Finding the man easy and resigned, Boswell, without in the least foregoing his warmest sympathy, considers 'how amazing it would be if a man under sentence of death should really laugh, and, with the nicest care of a diligent Student of human nature, I as decently as possible first smiled as he did, and gradually cherished the risible exertion, till he and I together fairly laughed.... It was truly a curious scene'.[1] Or again, to discover whether a streetwalker have any virtue, he leaves his friend, Mary, as much money as she says she can live on till his return, and then persuades two acquaintances to tempt her with large bribes to break her engagement in his absence 'and to write me what she did'.[2]

The same insatiable desire to see human nature subjected to stresses and tensions drew Boswell to all the executions within reach. Such occasions were for him

[1] *Private Papers*, VII, 152.   [2] Cf. *ibid*. VII, 156–157.

valuable opportunities to examine and compare the bared soul of another with what he found in his own breast. 'I never saw a man hanged but I thought I could behave better than he did, except Mr Gibson', he writes after one event of this kind.[1] In a similar spirit, Boswell went to see David Hume in his last illness, in order to try if the great atheist would falter when the shadow of death was upon him.

In his Commonplace-Book, Boswell once made a delightful remark that shows considerable self-knowledge:

> Boswell [he wrote], who had a good deal of whim, used not only to form wild projects in his imagination, but would sometimes reduce them to practice. In his calm hours, he said, with great good humour, 'There have been many people who built castles in the air, but I believe I am the first that ever attempted to live in them.'[2]

Of this romantic aspect of Boswell's character, and of his technique of social experimentation, Professor Tinker, who quotes the foregoing remark, has made an admirably discriminating analysis in his *Young Boswell*, and there is no need to cover the ground again. But Professor Tinker justly observes, in the light of Boswell's achievements, each of which was at the start 'a somewhat crackbrained dream', that

> it is important for those who call Boswell a fool to sit down and meditate on the whole nature of folly. Unless they are prepared to deny his genius altogether, they must realise that it was inseparably bound up with this romantic folly of his, which, when its airy castles prove to be of solid substance, has a very different look.[3]

VI

Such, then, are the elements that compose for Boswell the most intense and valuable experience: a vivid realization

[1] *Private Papers*, VII, 164.
[2] Quoted by C. B. Tinker, *Young Boswell*, Boston, 1922, p. 182.
[3] *Ibid*. pp. 183–184.

of the colour and quality of the moment, an awareness made more acute by comparison and contrast, an occasion that is in its own right rich in its revelation of human nature, and one that he has himself consciously helped to bring about.

If we look for a single episode to exhibit all these elements in their exaltation and to reveal the man himself in some of his most characteristic attitudes, we shall find it difficult to better the account of his first acquaintance with Rousseau.

Boswell had a letter of introduction to Rousseau which he was determined not to use, preferring to get into the great man's presence entirely by his own merits. Rousseau was at this time in bad health, and living in strictest seclusion at Val de Travers. Boswell put up at the village inn and sent Rousseau a letter in Boswellian French. In it he announced himself as a young Scot travelling for self-improvement, 'a man of unique merit,...with a sensitive heart, a spirit lively yet melancholy', whose sufferings give him a special title to Rousseau's consideration. Rousseau, who has so complete an insight into human nature, will not require an introduction; and Boswell submits himself to his severest scrutiny. 'Your writings, Sir, have softened my heart, raised my spirits, and kindled my imagination. Believe me, you will be glad to see me.... I have a presentiment that a noble friendship is to be born this day.' Rousseau must not let his illness prevent Boswell's reception. 'You will find in me a simplicity which will in no wise disturb you and a cordiality which may assist you in forgetting your pains.' He hints that he is a case for the specialist: 'I am in serious and delicate circumstances, and am most ardently desirous of having the counsels of the author of "La Nouvelle Heloise"....Open your door, then, Sir, to a man who dares to say that he deserves to enter there. Trust a unique foreigner. You will never repent it.'¹ The letter, as Boswell confided to his journal, 'can neither be abridged nor transposed, for it is realy a Master-Piece. I shall ever preserve it as a Proof that my Soul can be sublime'.² And later, to Temple, he wrote, 'No other man in Europe could have written such a letter, and appeared equal to all it's praise.'³ Boswell was upon the rack until word arrived that Rousseau would see him for a brief while. Thereupon, he records,

> To prepare myself for the great Interview, I walked out alone. ...The fresh, healthfull air and the romantic Prospect arround me gave me a vigourous and solemn tone. I recalled all my former ideas of J. J. Rousseau, the admiration with which he is regarded over all Europe, his *Heloise*, his *Emile*, in short, a crowd of great thoughts. This half hour was one of the most remarkable that I ever past.⁴

The interview passed off well. Rousseau received him without formality, wearing his customary Armenian dress:

> I was drest in a coat and Waistcoat, scarlet with Gold lace, Buckskin Breeches and Boots. Above all I wore a Great coat of Green Camlet lined with Fox-skin fur, with the collar and Cuffs of the same fur. I held under my arm a hat with a sollid gold lace, at least with the air of being sollid. . . . I had a free air and spoke well, and when M. Rousseau said what touched me more than ordinary, I seised his hand, I thumped him on the shoulder. I was without restraint.⁵

Boswell was admitted again the next day, and the next. At the third interview, he asked Rousseau to 'look after' him: a responsibility which Rousseau declined. Boswell was going to Môtiers for a fortnight. 'But I shall come back to you.' *Rousseau.* 'I don't promise to see you. I am ill. I need a chamber-pot every minute.' *Boswell.* 'Yes, you will see me!'⁶ Meanwhile, he leaves him a little

¹ *Young Boswell*, pp. 50–52. Professor Tinker's translation. The original French is in *Letters*, I, 58 ff.
² *Private Papers*, IV, 50.   ³ *Ibid.* IV, 14.
⁴ *Ibid.* IV, 55.   ⁵ *Ibid.* IV, 57.
⁶ *Ibid.* IV, 75.

sketch of his life, so that Rousseau may advise him the better. When he returns, Rousseau informs him that he has read the memoir.

Boswell. 'But can I yet hope to make something of myself?' *Rousseau.* 'Why, yes. Your great difficulty is that you think it so difficult a matter. Come back in the afternoon. But put your watch on the table.' *Boswell.* 'For how long?' *Rousseau.* 'A quarter of an hour, and no longer.' *Boswell.* 'Twenty minutes.' *Rousseau.* 'Be off with you!—Ha! Ha!' Notwithstanding the pain he was in, he was touched with my singular sally, and laughed most realy. He had a gay look immediatly.[1]

The fifth interview, then, took place at Rousseau's invitation. On this occasion, the two talk a good deal about women, and about the superiority of a life of virtue over one of sensuality. Boswell asks for advice on his future, and Rousseau tells him, if he wants to get on with his father, to develop a common amusement, like shooting; and, if he wants to get on in life, to stop taking other people's advice, to choose a profession and stick to it even if another one apparently better comes in sight. At last:

He stopped, and looked at me in a singular manner, 'Are you greedy?' *Boswell.* 'Yes.' *Rousseau.* 'I am sorry to hear it.' *Boswell.* 'Ha! Ha! I was joking; for in your books you write in favor of greed. I know what you are about to say, and it is just what I was hoping to hear. I wanted to solicit your soup. I had a great desire to share a meal with you.' *Rousseau.* 'Well, if you are not greedy, will you dine here tomorrow? But I give you fair warning, you will find yourself badly off.' *Boswell.* 'No, I shall not be badly off; I am above all such considerations.' *Rousseau.* 'Come then at noon; it will give us time to talk.' *Boswell.* 'All my thanks.'[2]

Early next morning, Boswell rides out on horseback to get himself in tune for the coming meal. He is delighted with the romantic scenery, and vastly elevated at the honour of Rousseau's invitation:

I was full of fine spirits. Gods! Am I now then realy the freind [*sic*] of Rousseau? What a rich assemblage of ideas! I relish my

[1] *Private Papers*, IV, 87, 89.　　　　[2] *Ibid.* IV, 95, 97.

felicity truly in such a scene as this. Shall I not truly relish it at Auchinleck? I was quite gay, my fancy was youthfull, and vented it's gladness in sportive sallies. I supposed myself in the rude world. I supposed a parcel of young fellows saying, 'Come, Boswell, you'll dine with us today?' 'No, Gentlemen, excuse me; I'm engaged. I dine today with Rousseau.' My tone, my air, my native Pride when I pronounced this![1]

The hour of luncheon approaches, and Boswell comes to the philosopher's door, vibrating in unison with the occasion. He finds Rousseau in good spirits. After the preliminaries, the conversation gets under way. Boswell's record of it is as follows:

I gave him very fully the character of Mr Johnson. He said with force, 'I would like that man. I would respect him. I would refrain from shattering his principles, were I to find I could do so. I should like to see him; but from far off for fear he might deal me a blow.'...I told him Mr Johnson's *Bon Mot* upon the Innovators: That Truth is a Cow which will yeild them no more Milk, and so they are gone to milk the Bull. He said, 'He would detest me. He would say, "Here is a Corrupter: a Man who comes here to milk the Bull".' I had diverted myself by pretending to help Mademoiselle Vasseur to make the Soup. We din'd in the Kitchen which was neat and chearfull. There was something singularly agreable in this scene. Here was Rousseau in all his Simplicity, with his Armenian dress which I have surely mentioned before now. His long coat and Nightcap made him look easy and well. Our dinner was as follows: 1 A dish of excellent Soup. 2 A Bouilli of Beef and Veal. 3 Cabbage, Turnip and Carrot. 4 Cold Pork. 5 Pickled Trout which he jestingly called *Tongue*. 6 Some little dish which I forget. The Desert consisted of stoned Pears and of Chesnuts. We had red and white wines. It was a simple good Repast. We were quite at our ease. I sometimes forgot myself and became ceremonious. 'May I help you to some of this dish?' *Rousseau*. 'No, Sir. I can help myself to it.' Or, 'Might I help myself to some more of that?' *Rousseau*. 'Is your arm long enough? A man does the honours of his house from a motive of vanity. He does not want it forgotten who is the Master. I would like everyone to be his own Master, and that no one should play the part of Host. Let each one ask for what he wants; if it is there to give, let him be given it;

---

[1] *Private Papers*, iv, 99.

otherwise, he must be satisfied without. Here you see true hospitality.'[1]

Boswell is much struck by this simplicity, and is led to make remarks upon it. Does it not, he asks, cheapen Rousseau in the eyes of others? Now the Scots, in their society, would at once take advantage of it.

Boswell. 'If you were in Scotland, they would start off by calling you "Rousseau, Jean Jacques, how goes it?" with the utmost familiarity.' *Rousseau.* 'That is perhaps a good thing.' *Boswell.* 'But they would say, "Poh, Jean Jacques, why do you allow yourself all these fantasies? You're a pretty man to put forward such claims. Come, Come, settle down in society like other people"; and this they will say to you with a sourness which, for my part, I am quite unable to imitate for you.' *Rousseau.* 'Ah, that's bad.' There he felt the thistle, when it was applied to himself on the tender part. It was just as if I had said, 'Howt Johnie Rousseau man, what for hae ye sae mony figmagairies? Ye're a bony Man indeed to mauk sicana wark; set ye up. Canna ye just live like ither fowk?'[2]

Boswell declares that, as for himself, he has leanings toward despotism, and at home on his estate does not allow his tenants much familiarity.

Rousseau. 'Do you like Cats?' *Boswell.* 'No.' *Rousseau.* 'I was sure of that. It is my test of character. There you have the despotic instinct of men. They do not like cats because the cat is free, and will never consent to become a slave. He will do nothing to your order, as the other animals do.'[3]

Boswell thinks of another exception: neither will chickens. The cat, replies Rousseau, will understand your wishes perfectly, yet refuse to obey. In spite of which, cats will be much attached to you, as independent friends. He shows Boswell his own dog and cat, and describes their play.

He put some victuals on a trencher, and made his dog dance round it. He sung to him a lively air with a sweet voice and great taste. 'You see the Ballet. It is not a gala performance, but a pretty

[1] *Private Papers*, IV, 101, 103.   [2] *Ibid.* IV, 105.
[3] *Ibid.* IV, 107.

one all the same.' I think the Dog's name was Sultan. He stroaked him and fed him, and with an arch air said, 'He is not much *respected*, but he gets well looked after.'[1]

The conversation then drifts from one topic to another: the English Church, Johnson's pension, Voltaire's dislike of Rousseau, Voltaire's Philosophical Dictionary. Of the last:

Rousseau. 'I don't like it. I am not intolerant, but he deserves... (I forget his expression here). It is very well to argue against men's opinion; But to show contempt, and to say, "You are idiots to believe this", is to be personally offensive. Now go away.' *Boswell.* 'Not yet. I will leave at three o'clock. I have still five and twenty minutes.' *Rousseau.* 'But I can't give you five and twenty minutes.' *Boswell.* 'I will give you even more than that.' *Rousseau.* 'What! Of my own time? All the Kings on earth cannot give me my own time.' *Boswell.* 'But if I had stayed till tomorrow I should have had five and twenty minutes, and next day another twenty-five. I am not taking these minutes. I am making you a present of them.' *Rousseau.* 'Ah! Since you don't steal my money, you are giving it to me.' He then repeated part of a french satire ending with, *and whatever they leave you, they count as a gift.* (Ce qu'ils ne vous prennent pas, ils disent qu'ils vous le donnent.)[2]

Boswell then appeals to Mademoiselle Le Vasseur. She promises to call when the clock strikes, and Rousseau is content. The two men walk up and down in the balcony in desultory conversation. Boswell will be happy to do anything for Rousseau in Italy, whither he is about to go; so Rousseau tells him he can pick up some pretty opera tunes to send back. When Mademoiselle Le Vasseur calls that Boswell's man is waiting outside,

M. Rousseau embraced me. He was quite the tender St Preux. He kist me several times, and held me in his arms with elegant cordiality. O! I shall never forget that I have been thus. *Rousseau.* 'Good-bye. You are a fine fellow.' *Boswell.* 'You have shown me great goodness, but I deserved it.' *Rousseau.* 'Yes. You are malicious; but 'tis a pleasant malice, a malice I don't dislike. Write and tell me how you are.' *Boswell.* 'And you will write to me?'

[1] *Private Papers,* IV, 107, 109.   [2] *Ibid.* IV, III.

Rousseau. 'I know not how to reach you.' *Boswell.* 'Yes, you shall write to me in Scotland.' *Rousseau.* 'Certainly; and even at Paris.' *Boswell.* 'Bravo! If I live twenty years, you will write to me for twenty years?' *Rousseau.* 'Yes.' *Boswell.* 'Good-bye. If you live for seven years, I shall return to Switzerland from Scotland to see you.' *Rousseau.* 'Do so. We shall be old acquaintances.' *Boswell.* 'One word more. Can I feel sure that I am held to you by the slenderest thread? By a hair?' (Seising a hair of my head.) *Rousseau.* 'Yes. Remember always that there are points where our souls are linked.' *Boswell.* 'It is enough. I, with my melancholy, I, who often look on myself as a despicable being, as a good for nothing creature who should make his escape from life,—I shall be upheld forever by the thought that I am linked to M. Rousseau. Good-bye. Bravo! I will live to the end of my days.' *Rousseau.* 'That is undoubtedly a thing one must do. Good-bye.'[1]

Boswell then takes leave of Mademoiselle Le Vasseur, and promises to send her a garnet necklace. She says she told Rousseau at Boswell's first appearance that he had an honest face, and declares that already Rousseau has a 'high regard' for him. And she waves him good-bye as he rides away.

In this little chronicle almost every characteristic mark of Boswell's genius is to be seen: his fantastic imagination, his illimitable cheek, his consuming egoism, his disarming friendliness and good humour, his pathetic insufficiency and desire for authority, his curiosity about human nature, and, finally, his faculty of lively perception and enormous zest for life.

VII

His deepest literary instincts are merely the unassuming bondservants of these qualities. Essentially, his interest is not literary. The combination of his desire for self-improvement and his relish of existence compels him to preserve all he can of experience, and he does his best to get a lasting impression of the days as they pass over him.

[1] *Private Papers*, IV, 113, 115.

His achievement, notable as it is, falls far short of his ideal. For his ideal is to fix life itself, the actual living; and he acknowledges that what he can do is a poor substitute for that actuality. The evanescent fluctuations of feeling cannot be caught. Whilst the art of the portrait painter can seize the traits of character in a face, and musical sounds can adequately convey the intentions of the composer, the varieties of mind elude, Boswell thinks, the words which must embody them. 'We must be content to enjoy the recollection of characters in our own breasts.'[1]

Words are insufficient; but words are yet curiously potent in Boswell's hands. With the minimum appearance of conscious effort either for selection of the just expression or for the disposition of phrases in gratifying cadences, his unassuming style does marvellously well in communicating his sense of eager life, the quality of sensuous experience. He seldom misses fire or has to try a second time, and he contrives with Scottish frugality to make a little go a long way. Consider the evocative power of the following simple statement:

This morning I was in delicious spirits. I stood calm in my chamber, while the Sun shone sweet upon me, and was sure that after gloom I may be quite well.[2]

If one venture to touch this unstudied excellence with the rude hand of analysis, it will be found, I suspect, that its whole virtue lives in three adjectives. Substitute other expressions for the words, *delicious, calm, sweet*, and the magic fades. The words are common enough, but another temperament would not have dictated their use in this context. In particular, *calm*—along with *firm, solid, solemn*, and *fine*—falls into the most connotative portion of Boswell's private vocabulary.

[1] *Private Papers*, x, 244. Cf. also *ibid.* viii, 60.
[2] *Ibid.* iii, 123.

Sometimes a single felicitous word will evoke a whole scene. When Boswell had got Johnson to Edinburgh in August, 1773, and was showing him the 'Laigh' Parliament House, or Scottish Record Office, he wrote: 'I was pleased to behold Dr Samuel Johnson rolling about in this old magazine of antiquities.'[1]

His style at its best has an unselfconscious directness that can only be compared to folk poetry. A passage which strikingly illustrates the simplicity, as well as the 'happy valiancy', of Boswell's rendition of experience, is the following, of March 19, 1768:

We got to York at night and put up at Bluitt's Inn. We were dusty, bustling fellows, and no sooner was our baggage taken off than we posted to the Theatre. We went into the back seat of one of the boxes, and indeed there was a pretty company. I loved to see so many genteel people in their own county town, in place of crowding to London. The Play was *False Delicacy*, and the farce, *A Peep behind the curtain*. Wilkinson, the Mimick, played, and several of the Performers did very well. We returned to our Inn and had an excellent supper....I never saw a better Inn. The waiters had all one Livery; brown coats and scarlet vests. We had hitherto been raised very early; but we now resolved to take sufficient repose for a night. Upon my word, eating, drinking, and sleeping are matters of great moment.[2]

If Boswell complained that the 'peculiar features of mind which distinguish individuals' escaped being subjected to words, he had little reason to feel dissatisfied with his power to seize and fix *external* features. An album of vivid portraits could be culled from his writings. His photographic memory holds the image before his mind while in two or three descriptive phrases he hastily sets down in his journal the essential appearance. Raeburn could have painted a masterpiece from the following note:

Kingsburgh was completely the figure of a gallant Highlander. ...He had his Tartan plaid thrown about him, a large blue bonnet

[1] *Tour*, ed. Chapman, 1930, p. 184.
[2] *Private Papers*, VII, 159–160.

with a knot of black ribband like a cockade, a brown short coat of a kind of duffil, a Tartan waistcoat with gold buttons and gold button-holes, a bluish philibeg, and Tartan hose. He had jet black hair tied behind, [with screwed ringlets on each side,] and was a large stately man, with a steady sensible countenance.[1]

But Boswell is not content until action and dialogue are added to bring the picture to life:

> We paid a visit to the Reverend Mr Hector M'Lean.... He was about seventy-seven years of age, a decent ecclesiastick, dressed in a full suit of black clothes, and a black wig.... It was curious to see him and Dr Johnson together. Neither of them heard very distinctly; so each of them talked in his own way, and at the same time. Mr M'Lean said, he had a confutation of Bayle, by Leibnitz.— *Johnson.* 'A confutation of Bayle, sir! What part of Bayle do you mean? The greatest part of his writings is not confutable: it is historical and critical.'—Mr M'Lean said, 'the irreligious part;' and proceeded to talk of Leibnitz's controversy with Clarke, calling Leibnitz a great man.—*Johnson.* 'Why, sir, Leibnitz persisted in affirming that Newton called space *sensorium numinis*, notwithstanding he was corrected, and desired to observe that Newton's words were QUASI *sensorium numinis*. No, sir; Leibnitz was as paltry a fellow as I know. Out of respect to Queen Caroline, who patronised him, Clarke treated him too well.'
>
> During the time that Dr Johnson was thus going on, the old minister was standing with his back to the fire, cresting up erect, pulling down the front of his periwig, and talking what a great man Leibnitz was. To give an idea of the scene, would require a page with two columns; but it ought rather to be represented by two good players.[2]

In this way the 'great lines of characters', as Boswell phrases it, might be put upon the page. But how to bridge the gap between the record and life itself? Since the gulf could never be crossed until such time as words should become the equivalent of sensations, what was the best that could be done? Working on such materials in a medium so imperfect, one was not even within striking

[1] *Tour*, p. 279. The phrase in brackets is in the original diary: cf. *Boswell's Journal of a Tour to the Hebrides*, ed. F. A. Pottle and C. H. Bennett, New York, 1936, p. 159.

[2] *Tour*, ed. Chapman, p. 352–353.

distance of the point at which the real technical problems of literary art might arise. It was obvious, meanwhile, that the fuller the record the closer would be the approximation to the richness of actual experience. The more 'variations of mind', the more 'workings of reason and passion', the more 'colourings of fancy' one could crowd into the register, the more completely (though forever imperfectly) would living, itself, be mirrored. The primary rule, therefore, for biography, as for autobiography, was the rule of inclusion. 'Indeed,' Boswell wrote at the commencement of his *Life of Johnson*,

I cannot conceive a more perfect mode of writing any man's life, than not only relating all the most important events of it in their order, but interweaving what he privately wrote, and said, and thought; by which mankind are enabled as it were to see him live, and to 'live o'er each scene' with him, as he actually advanced through the several stages of his life.[1]

To see the man live, to live each scene with him: that was the Boswellian ideal. Even dimly to realize it, one must have kept such a record as Boswell's journal contained of his own day-to-day existence. His autobiography is probably the nearest approach to that ideal which has ever been penned. Next after it comes the *Life of Johnson*. But the latter could not have been written without the autobiography to draw upon. For the feature of the *Life* which brings it closest to the ideal, and which sets it at one stride immeasurably ahead of all other biographies, is, as everyone recognizes, the *scenes* which we relive with Boswell in Johnson's company. And these scenes were originally recorded as parts of Boswell's autobiography, not of the *Life*.

With the publication of the Journals, we know at last exactly what happened in the translation from the Boswell-record to the Johnson-record. The original materials were

---

[1] *Life*, I, 30.

treated with scrupulous fidelity. But at many points, vivid as the *Life* is, the primary document, with the lens focused upon Boswell himself, gives us an even more intense and richer actuality. It is something to be told, in the *Life*, that when Boswell returned to Johnson from abroad, 'he received me with much kindness'; but better to learn: 'You kneel'd, and ask'd his blessing...he hug'd you to him like a sack, and grumbl'd, "I hope we shall pass many years of regard together".'[1]

One could not ask a finer opportunity for a comparative view of the two records at a point of convergence than the parallel accounts of the visit to Oxford in the spring of 1768. The Journal leads off with matter not included in the *Life*:

(26 March, 1768.) I...set out early this morning in the Oxford Fly. Anthony had an outside place. My travelling companions were an old redfaced fat Gentlewoman who lived in the Borough of Southwark, and whose Husband dealt in a wholesale trade of brandy and wine. Dr Cockayne, a lecturer at one of the Churches, lodged in her house, having his own maid servant and a Boy. But she would not board the Doctor. 'No, no. I knows him too well. Why, he's the greatest Epicure, perpetually minding his belly. I tells him, "Why, Doctor, you do nothing else from morning to night. You sure have a false pocket." And so I roasts him. But he's a good-natured creature, and would have every one to share with him. He gets up my daughter, "Come now, Miss, we'll have some tea and something very nice with it".' Besides this good woman, there was a Clergyman, a stiff divine, a fellow of a college in Oxford. He was very wise and laughed at the old Lady. The fourth in the coach was a little Taylour who has often tripped over to France and Flanders, and who therefore had a right to talk as a travelled man. All the road was roaring with 'Wilkes and Liberty', which, with 'No. 45', was chalked on every coach and chaise. We breakfasted at Slow. We became very merry. We dined at Henley, and there we were as hearty as People could be. We had a good drive to Oxford with allways t'other joke on Dr Cockayne. We stopped at the gate of Magdalen College, of which our Clergyman was a fellow. He jumped out of the coach, and in a moment

---

[1] *Private Papers*, VII, 68; *Life*, II, 5.

we saw what a great man he was; for he went into the Barber's and got the key of his chambers, and two or three people followed him with his trunk, tea things, and I know not what all. The Lady left us here too. The Taylour and I put up at the Angel, where the Coach inns; but we parted there. I immediatly had some coffee and then got a guide to shew me New Inn Hall. Mr Johnson lived in the house of Mr Chambers, the head of that hall and Vinerian Professour at Oxford. I supposed the Professour would be very formal and I apprehended but an aukward reception. However, I rung and was shewn into the Parlour. In a little, down came Mr Chambers, a lively, easy, agreable Newcastle man. I had sent up my name, 'Mr Boswell'. After receiving me very politely, 'Sir', said he, 'you are Mr Boswell of Auchinleck?' 'Yes, Sir.' 'Mr Johnson wrote to you yesterday. He dined abroad, but I expect him in every minute.' 'Oho!' thought I, 'this is excellent.' I was quite relieved. Mr Cha[mb]ers gave me tea, and by and by arrived the great man. He took me all in his arms and kist me on both sides of the head, and was as cordial as ever I saw him. I told him all my perplexity on his account, and how I had come determined to fight him, or to do any thing he pleased. [Boswell knew that Johnson was irritated by his having published without permission, in his *Corsica*, part of the Doctor's correspondence with him.] 'What', said he, 'did you come here on purpose?' 'Yes, indeed', said I. This gave him high satisfaction. I told him how I was settled as a Lawyer and how I had made 200 Pounds by the law this year. He grumbled and laughed and was wonderfully pleased. 'What, Bosy? two hundred pounds! A great deal.' I had longed much to see him as my great Preceptour, to state to him some difficulties as a moralist with regard to the Profession of the law, as it appeared to me that in some respects it hurt the principles of honesty, and I asked him if it did not.[1]

At this point the two records coalesce, and there follows, with a few slight verbal differences, a paragraph which may be given as it stands in the *Life*:

JOHNSON. 'Why no, Sir, if you act properly. You are not to deceive your clients with false representations of your opinion: you are not to tell lies to a judge.' BOSWELL. 'But what do you think of supporting a cause which you know to be bad?' JOHNSON. 'Sir, you do not know it to be good or bad till the Judge determines it. I have said that you are to state facts fairly; so that your thinking, or what

[1] *Private Papers*, VII, 168–169.

you call knowing, a cause to be bad, must be from reasoning, must be from your supposing your arguments to be weak and inconclusive. But, Sir, that is not enough. An argument which does not convince yourself, may convince the Judge to whom you urge it: and if it does convince him, why, then, Sir, you are wrong, and he is right. It is his business to judge; and you are not to be confident in your own opinion that a cause is bad, but to say all you can for your client, and then hear the Judge's opinion.' BOSWELL. 'But, Sir, does not affecting a warmth when you have no warmth, and appearing to be clearly of one opinion when you are in reality of another opinion, does not such dissimulation impair one's honesty? Is there not some danger that a lawyer may put on the same mask in common life, in the intercourse with his friends?' JOHNSON. 'Why no, Sir. Every body knows you are paid for affecting warmth for your client; and it is, therefore, properly no dissimulation: the moment you come from the bar you resume your usual behaviour. Sir, a man will no more carry the artifice of the bar into the common intercourse of society, than a man who is paid for tumbling upon his hands will continue to tumble upon his hands when he should walk on his feet.'[1]

In the Journal—not in the *Life*—Boswell continues as follows:

Wonderful force and fancy. At once he satisfied me as to a thing which had often and often perplexed me. It was truly comfortable having him in his old high-church oxford, and I had besides many good ideas of the Vinerian Professour, the head of a Hall, etc.... I told Mr Johnson a story which I should have recorded before this time. The day before I left London, coming through Bloomsbury Square and being drest in green and gold, I was actually taken for Wilkes by a Middlesex voter who came up to me. 'Sir, I beg pardon, is not your name Wilkes?' 'Yes, Sir.' 'I thought so. I saw you upon the hustings and I thought I knew you again. Sir, I'm your very good friend; I've got you five and twenty votes today.' I bow'd and grin'd and thanked him and talked of Liberty and General Warrants and I don't know what all. I told him too, between ourselves, that the King had a very good opinion of me. I ventured to ask him how he could be sure that I was a right man and acted from publick spirit. He was a little puzzled. So I helped him out. 'As to my private character, it would take a long time to explain it. But, Sir, if I were the Devil, I have done good to the People of England, and they ought to support me.' 'Ay,' said he.

[1] *Life*, II, 47–48.

I am vexed I did not make more of this curious incident. After carrying my voter half way down Long Acre, I stopped and looked him gravely in the face. 'Sir, I must tell you a secret. I'm not Mr Wilkes, and what's more I'm a Scotsman.' He started not a little, and said, 'Sir, I beg pardon for having given you so much trouble.' 'No, Sir,' said I, 'you have been very good company to me.' I wonder he did not beat me. I said to Mr Johnson that I never before knew that I was so ugly a fellow. He was angry at me that I did not borrow money from the voter. Indeed it would have made a fine scene at Brentford when he demanded payment of the real Wilkes, and called him a Rogue for denying the debt.[1]

The conversation then turns upon various authors, as in the *Life*, except that there Boswell introduces pertinent remarks of the Doctor made at other times, to illustrate what he now says. Johnson makes a cursory distinction between spontaneous and solicited testimony, with the following example:

If I praise a man's book without being asked my opinion of it, that is honest praise, to which one may trust. But if an authour asks me if I like his book, and I give him something like praise, it must not be taken as my real opinion.[2]

Boswell, who is in a fever of impatience to know what Johnson thinks about his *Corsica*, reflects, 'I should not ask him about my Book.' The conversation then proceeds as reported in the *Life*. When the company breaks up, Boswell goes to bed with comfortable thoughts of the agreeable contrast between this and the London nights preceding it.

On the following evening, Boswell gives a supper party at the Angel for Dr Johnson and Professor Chambers. He allows a young Christ Church man, an undergraduate with whom he has had breakfast, to attend, 'upon his promising to be very quiet and submissive'. The guests assemble at nine, and Boswell gives them a good supper, with madeira and warm port negus. The conversation

---

[1] *Private Papers*, VII, 170–171.
[2] *Life*, II, 51. *Private Papers*, VII, 172.

proceeds as in the *Life*, Johnson expatiating on the advantages of Oxford as a place of learning—in the Journal, Boswell inserts his own reactions to these remarks—and going on to other topics and personalities. The Journal supplies identifications and lacks the discretion of the published account.

He was very hard on poor Dr Blair, whom he holds wonderfully cheap for having written a Dissertation on Ossian. Talking of the future life of Brutes, 'Sir', said he, 'if you allow Blair's soul to be immortal, why not allow a Dog to be imortal?' I wanted much to defend the pleasing system of Brutes existing in the other world. Mr Johnson, who does not like to hear any ideas of futurity but what are in the Thirty nine Articles, was out of humour with me, and watched his time to give me a blow. So when I, with a serious, metaphysical, pensive face, ventured to say, 'But really, Sir, when we see a very sensible dog, we know not what to think of him', he turned about, and growling with joy replied, 'No, Sir; and when we see a very foolish fellow, we don't know what to think of him.' Then up he got, bounced along, and stood by the fire, laughing and exulting over me. . . . About twelve they left me.[1]

The rest of the conversation reported in the *Life* took place next day, some of it after breakfast, some in the evening. The topics cover a considerable range, from whether the scorpion stings himself to death, and from the conglobulation of swallows, to travel books and the question of female virtue. While Johnson is enforcing the principle of chastity, Boswell, as we learn from the Journal,

argued that virtue might be found even in a common street walker. [Perhaps he is thinking of Mary, back in Edinburgh.] He laughed, and as I had told him of my dutch lady [Zélide], 'Why, (said he,) I shall have the dutch Lady; you can get a wife in the streets.'[2]

Since Zélide has been mentioned, Boswell expresses his fears that she is too brilliant for him. This topic is discreetly handled in the *Life*:

A gentleman talked to him of a lady whom he greatly admired and wished to marry, but was afraid of her superiority of talents.

[1] *Private Papers*, VII, 176.   [2] *Ibid*. VII, 179.

'Sir, (said he,) you need not be afraid; marry her. Before a year goes about, you'll find that reason much weaker, and that wit not so bright.'[1]

Soon after, Boswell's guests depart, and he concludes his account in the Journal thus:

This was another good night. How different was I from what I was when I last saw Mr Johnson in London, when I was still wavering, and often clouded. I am now serene and steady. I took leave of the company, being to set out next morning.[2]

Thus, with 'prompt assiduity' and with unflagging interest, Boswell traced his own and Johnson's earthly course, and fashioned his immortal record.

The motto on Boswell's crest was 'Vraye Foy'. Whether we think of the man's strenuous and lifelong effort to know himself, and honestly to acknowledge in writing whatever self-scrutiny revealed; or whether we contemplate that segment of human experience preserved in the Journals, the *Tour*, and the *Life of Johnson*—the unparalleled reality, the unrivalled veracity of that record: we must surely allow that James Boswell, in his appointed, inimitable way, made good his title to the sign he bore— *Vraye Foy*.

[1] *Life*, II, 56–57.   [2] *Private Papers*, VII, 179.

JOHNSON'S 'IRENE'

VARIATIONS ON A TRAGIC THEME

I. THE BACKGROUND

Bandello first drew Irene from the ocean of oral tradition on to the *terra firma* of print. Her history formed the tenth novel of his collection, published in 1554. Within five years men were reading about her in Boaistuau's French, and in 1566 Painter printed an English version of the tale. Not many years later, George Peele gave it dramatic form, in 'the famous play of the Turkish Mahamet and Hyrin the fair Greek', with which Ancient Pistol had soon familiarized himself; but few could follow him, for it has unfortunately been lost to posterity. The story appeared in Latin chronicles in the fifteen-eighties and -nineties, and in 1603 Richard Knolles gave it dignified place in his monumental *Historie of the Turks*.

Knolles disapproves of the tyrant, Mahomet II, 'the Great', and all his works and ways; but he has the states-man's point of view. Without pausing to consider what further mischief Irene might be hindering Mahomet from committing, he regards the latter's infatuation as a malady. 'All the day he spent with her in discourse, and the night in daliance: all time spent in her companie, seemed vnto him short; and without her nothing pleased: his fierce nature was now by her well tamed, and his wonted care of armes quite neglected: *Mars* slept in *Venus* lap, and now the soldiors might go play....Such is the power of dis-ordered affections, where reason ruleth not the reine.'[1]

When Mahomet is warned, by his trusted friend Mustapha, of the dangerous discontent of his officers and

[1] For notes see pages 154–155.

soldiers, he is sorely vexed: 'reason calling vpon him, for his honour, and his amorous affections, still suggesting vnto him new delights. Thus tossed too and fro...hee resolued vpon a strange point, whereby at once to cut off all those his troubled passions; and withall, to strike a terrour euen into the stoutest of them that had before condemned him, as vnable to gouerne his owne so passionate affections'.[2] He devotes the next twenty-four hours solely to Irene, honouring and exalting her more than ever before. Then, having called a council of state, he brings the lady forth, and all complaints are hushed by her incomparable beauty. But 'presently with one of his hands catching the faire Greeke by the haire of the head, and drawing his falchion with the other, at one blow [he] strucke off her head, to the great terror of them all. And hauing so done, said vnto them: *Now by this iudge whether your emperour is able to bridle his affections or not.*'[3]

Knolles's whole interest is in Mahomet. Irene is a desperate disease which, having caught, the tyrant desperately cures. True, she is a paragon 'of such incomparable beautie and rare perfection, both of body & mind, as if nature had in her to the admiration of the world, laboured to haue showne her greatest skill'; but she has no more character than the mathematical symbol *pi*. She has no previous history, presents no opposition to her lover; and for only one moment does Knolles look on her as a human being. Mahomet commands her, on the last day, to be sumptuously attired. 'Whereunto the poore soule gladly obeyed, little thinking that it was her funerall apparell.' The phrase was caught directly from Painter, who got it from Boaistuau and Bandello ('non sapendo la miserella che apparecchiava i suoi funerali').

Presumably she had more personality in Peele's drama. At any rate, she comes alive in the first extant play on the subject, Gilbert Swinhoe's *Tragedy of the unhappy Fair*

Irene, 1658. Here she displays nobility, loyalty, and passion. In this version she acquires a husband, to whom she is devoted, and the interest turns on whether she will be able to keep Mahomet off by delays and seeming complaisance until her husband can rescue her. She manages the delay, but a tragic dénouement nevertheless ensues. The soldiers beset Mahomet's palace and force the gates. Irene faints with terror, and Mahomet, to prevent others from laying violent hands upon her, beheads her before she can regain consciousness. There are other points to be noted, in view of Johnson's later handling of the story. Her husband has a loyal friend, and in disguise they both gain access to her during her captivity. A good deal, in several scenes, is made of the grumbling of Janizaries and Bashaws before the final uprising. Natolia, who combines the roles of Johnson's (and Knolles's) Cali Bassa and Mustapha, but who in Swinhoe is loyal to his master, has a soliloquy that presents correspondences—though no significance need be attached thereto—with one in Johnson. Here are the parallels:

[Swinhoe:]
NATOLIA. Oh! How the Bark of Greatness rides on a rotten Cable,
Subject to every flaw of malice,
And impetuous Billow of Rebellion;
Our mighty Prince, but now,
Rid on the neck of an imperial Conquest:
But oh! one fatal change: he's pul'd from thence
By the seducing Charms of whining love;
And, in a probability, of reducement into nothing,
To have his awful Majesty flouted by common slaves....
[p. 21]

[Johnson:]
CALI. How Heav'n in Scorn of human Arrogance,
Commits to trivial Chance the Fate of Nations!
While with incessant Thought laborious Man
Extends his mighty Schemes of Wealth and Pow'r,
And tow'rs and triumphs in ideal Greatness;

Some accidental Gust of Opposition
Blasts all the Beauties of his new Creation,
O'erturns the Fabrick of presumptuous Reason,
And whelms the swelling Architect beneath it.   [ii, iii, 1–9]

And similar reflections upon the liability of greatness to disaster from petty causes are voiced at a similar moment by Mustapha, in the next play after Swinhoe's to deal with the subject: *Irena, A Tragedy*, 1664.

MUSTAPHA. What strange Fate attends on Princes actions?
Who would have thought this *Sultan*, lately ador'd
By these Perfidious Bassa's as if he
Had been some Deity, (and to whom they
Are beholding for all their present greatness)
Should so by one weak action, make 'em lose
The good opinion they had of him,
As that they now dare take up arms against him!. . .
                                        [i, iii; p. 13]

The anonymous author of 1664 improves upon the hints which Swinhoe had thrown out to diversify and enrich the interest of the story. In fact, he has written a highly amusing, not in the least tragic, play of the Love-and-Honour class. He is fully aware of previous handlings of the story, and labours to explain motives and divergences. There is a great deal (far too much, in fact) of pure narrative in his version. The principals, at a bound, become ideal Restoration courtiers and ladies. All is lofty, if not in Ercles's vein. High-flown sentiment is the element in which everything floats.

The notable points about *Irena* are these. The heart interest is multiplied and magnified. Irena is not already married—during the half-dozen years since Swinhoe's play, it had, as everyone knows, become impossible for a wife to love her husband: instead, she has a lover, a brave Greek general. She also has a confidante in her captivity, a fellow captive whose heart is similarly engaged to a Greek captain. They suppose their lovers dead, but resolve to be true to their memories. Irena's devotion keeps her unmoved by the thought of power which Mahomet's love offers her. The lovers (old friends, of course) gain secret access to the palace gardens and reveal themselves to the ladies, whose faithful protestations they overhear and break in upon. Measures for escape are concerted, a vessel lying in wait for that purpose. But first there are long expository speeches wherein the four bring one another *au courant* as to their private histories. Thus, Justinianus, Irena's lover, explains that he has met with mercy and courtesy in a Janizary who not only saved his life but gave him his liberty—a point both looking back to a courteous captain in Swinhoe and forward to the Caraza-Demetrius connection in Johnson. Justinianus also explains, contrary to the account in Knolles (who holds him personally responsible for the fall of Constantinople by his cowardly withdrawal in a crisis), that he had only momentarily retired, by his friends' persuasion, to get his wounds dressed, and had immediately returned to the breach.

In this play Mahomet proves himself the very pink of politeness and the flower of magnanimity. Like Johnson's Mahomet, he is astounded at the change in himself and at the power Irena has over him. He confesses he so stands in awe of her as not to dare enforce his will upon her. Learning of the conspiracy of his soldiers to do away with Irena, he soliloquizes:

> Love, and Ambition agitates my mind
> With equal Fury, And like to two
> Impetuous winds, when they meet together
> I'the Ocean, Each strives for mast'ry.
> State-Int'rest say's, Ambition here should sway
> > [*Pointing to his breast.*
> But Honour say's, That Love I should obey.
> For I'm oblig'd by Honour to protect
> *Irena*, though she does my Love neglect.
> Love gains the field in this contentious strife;
> 'Ile save *Irena*, or I'le lose my life.   [IV, i.; p. 53]

Later, he tries to induce her to fly with him—from his own soldiers!—but she is naturally inflexible, and would persuade him to leave her. He replies:

> Leave you *Irena*! no, that cannot be;
> If you miscarry, What becomes of me?   [p. 57]

She appeals to his ambition, and tries to screw up his spirits with some fine speeches. Love, she says, is a passion unworthy so great a mind. But he disagrees:

> Love's a Passion we too often find,
> That lodges most within a gen'rous mind.   [p. 59]

The fifth act is sufficiently busy. While the soldiers are storming the palace, Mahomet returns to the garden for another attempt to persuade Irena to fly, under his protection. He surprises the lovers in a rendezvous arranging their flight. This unsettles him; but meanwhile his Aga—who corresponds to Johnson's Cali—is prowling the garden with intent to kill him, a purpose which is about to be fulfilled when Justinianus pounces upon the Aga and saves Mahomet's life. Seeing the matter in this fresh view, Mahomet steps aside for a brief struggle between his more magnanimous instincts and his desire for Irena. The better part prevails and he determines upon yielding the lady to Justinianus. But at this point the Bassas storming the gates make good their entrance. There is hardly a moment to lose. Justinianus and his friend, who have had a band of five hundred hardy followers waiting outside to effect their own entrance and carry off the ladies, now offer their services to Mahomet against the Bassas. The lucky offer is accepted and they go to head their band. Mahomet hides the ladies in a handy secret vault in the garden, and causes Mustapha to dress a female slave so as to bring out her naturally striking resemblance to Irena. When the Bassas burst into the garden, Mahomet appears on a balcony with this slave, makes a speech to them (as in Knolles), and suddenly stabs the slave, whom they take to be really Irena. Having thus won their point, the Bassas yield submission; Justinianus breaks through with his followers to clinch matters; the ladies are exhumed from the vault; the murder is softened by the information that the slave impersonating Irena had already been condemned to execution for a 'notorious crime'; the Sultan makes formal presentation of the two ladies to their respective lovers, and all ends with mutual compliment and thanks. According to the Prologue, the author writ

> Not to gain praise, or to be call'd a wit,

but only to give delight; and the Epilogue appeals to the ladies to judge:

> He writ it to please you.

In the next play to be considered, *Irene; or the Fair Greek*, a tragedy by Charles Goring, 1708, Irene sinks back into a static rôle. She has already become Mahomet's mistress before the beginning of the play, is heavy with shame, and devotes herself chiefly to self-reproach for taking an infidel to her embrace:

> My Countries Plague! My Faith's inveterate Foe!
> Horrid with Stains of all my slaughter'd Race!

Aratus, a captive Prince of Corinth, has been her betrothed; but, though she still loves him and he her, he can make no headway, either to avenge her shame by killing Mahomet, or to carry her off by flight. Her objection to the latter course is that her pollution would blemish his name; but he believes there is another reason, and jealousy invades him. Mahomet, meanwhile, is moping with unrequited love, and determines to make Irene empress in order to win her heart. Pressure is brought upon him, however, by three loyal friends, to resume his martial pursuits. The friends anger him by their plain speech; they are condemned and imprisoned, but later reconciled and forgiven. At the Coronation Scene, Mahomet acts much as in Knolles, stabbing his Queen after his followers have approved his devotion to her. She is long a-dying, and Mahomet droops with love and remorse. After last-minute complications involving two additional deaths, Mahomet sums it all up in words which close the play:

> Jealous of Empire, and my lost Renown,
> I stabb'd a Mistress to preserve my Crown:
> But had the Fair return'd my generous Flame,
> I'd slighted Empire, and embrac'd the DAME.[4]

Goring has also invented a brother of Irene, Pyrrhus, whose chief importance for us lies in the fact that he introduces the note of apostasy. He has become a favourite of Mahomet, and for that reason flinches at Aratus's and his own joint design to murder the Sultan. At the end of the play, he commits suicide out of religious remorse:

> Yet Mercy, Heav'n, since thus my Blood I've spilt
> Rather than live in my Apostate Guilt.   [p. 57]

Aratus, who throughout has something of Johnson's fiery Abdalla, tries to kill Mahomet at the Coronation Scene. He is disarmed, but Mahomet, discovering that he had been Irene's betrothed, condescends to duel with him as man to man, and kills him in fair fight.[5] It should be added, finally, that Irene has a confidante, Zaida, of no importance in herself; and that the play is the only one so far—barring, perhaps, the lost one of Peele—to be in blank verse.[6]

These, then, are the English models available to Johnson, should he wish to make use of them. On the question of indebtedness, it will be well to quote Nichol Smith's remarks:

The interest of these plays lies mainly, and to the reader of Johnson perhaps wholly, in the treatment of the central figure.

There is no question of borrowing. None of them owes anything to another, nor did they provide anything to their greater successor. The two earlier plays Johnson may be assumed not to have known; if he happened to know the third, he certainly took nothing from it. Here are four independent renderings of Knolles's story, and four distinct presentations of the character of Irene.[7]

With proper respect to a distinguished scholar, these conclusions seem over-hasty.

Without intending to belabour the argument, we must review the ground travelled to see what has been gained. There is no doubt of Johnson's primary debt to Knolles. Besides his declared admiration of that work, there are specific page references to it, for various details, in the first draft of *Irene*. Numerous touches point the obligation. Thus, Knolles strongly enforces the corruption and venality of the defenders of Constantinople, stressed by Johnson at the opening of his play. Mahomet's covert hatred of Cali, in the play, is similarly motivated in Knolles; and Cali's connivance with the enemy, as also its discovery, are likewise in Knolles. Further evidence is of course abundant.

If the interest of the earlier plays lies chiefly in the treatment of Irene herself, it must be emphasized that neither they nor Johnson got any assistance in interpretation from Knolles's account of her. But here it is worth observing that there is in Knolles another story, with interesting similarities, of a beautiful Greek captive, to whom Knolles devotes much more sympathetic attention than he does to Irene. There are in all Knolles's thousand folio pages only three outstanding women: Irene, Roxolana, and Manto the wife of the great Bassa Ionuses. Manto has never received any notice from students of Johnson and for that reason it is desirable to quote her story. It is not easily missed by the desultory reader, for a full spread of the book is given over to medallion portraits of her and her husband, on opposite pages, with verses beneath each one, in Latin and English. Anyone except the source hunter would pause over these. Under Manto's picture Knolles's verses are as follows.

> Formam si spectes, nihil est formosius ista:
>   Pectoris & casti gratia rara fuit.
> Sed dum dissimili vixit malè iuncta marito:
>   Infelix misera morte perempta iacet.[8]

Ionuses was Bassa of Egypt about 1520, and he appears in the chronicle of Selymus the First. 'This great Bassa', writes Knolles,

in nothing so much offended the minds of the people (who generally both loued and honoured him) as by the crueltie by him shewed vpon the person of the faire ladie *Manto* his best beloued wife. Who being a Greek borne, and adorned with all the good gifts of nature, wherunto her louely conditions were also answerable, was by *Zebalia* her first husband (a man of great honour) carried with him into the wars, as his greatest treasure and chiefe delight. But he slaine, and she by misfortune falling into the hands of the Turks (her enemies) remained so prisoner with them for a time; vntill that this great Bassa *Ionuses* shortly after (seeing her amongst the other captiues there taken, so farre to exceed the rest as doth the Sunne the lesser stars) surprised with her incomparable beautie, became of her amorous: and in too curious viewing of the captiue ladie, was by her himselfe taken prisoner. Where finding her outward perfections graced with no lesse inward vertues, and her honourable mind answerable vnto her rare feature, tooke her vnto his wife; honouring her farre aboue all the rest of his wiues and concubines: and she againe in all dutifull loyaltie seeking to please him, for a space liued in all worldly felicitie and blisse, not much inferiour vnto one of the great Sultanesses. But long lasteth not the sommer fruit of wanton loue, blasted most times in the blossome, and rotten before it be well gathered: For in short time, the Bassa more amorous of her person than secured in her vertues, and after the manner of sensuall men still fearing least that which so much pleased himselfe, gaue no lesse contentment to others also; began to haue her in distrust, although he saw no great cause why, more than his owne conceit, not grounded vpon any her euill demeanor, but vpon the excesse of his owne liking. Which mad humour (hardly to be euer purged) of it selfe still more and more in him encreasing,

he became so froward and imperious, that nothing she could say
or doe could now so please or content him, but that he still thought
some one or other, although he wist not who, to be therein par-
takers with him. So fearfull was the jealous man of his owne
conceits. Yet could he not chuse but loue those great perfections,
whereat he could not enough wonder; although he found no contentment therein, tormenting still both himselfe and her whom he
so deerely loued with his owne passionat distrust: vntill at length,
the faire ladie grieued to see her selfe thus without cause to be
suspected, & wearied with the insolent pride of her peeuish husband,
togither with his imperious commands; determined secretly to
depart from him, and so to returne againe into her own country.
Which her purpose she discouered vnto one of her eunuchs, to
whom she had also deliuered certaine letters to be by him conuaied
vnto such of her friends, as whose helpe she was to vse in her intended flight: which letters the false eunuch opened, and so for the
more manifesting of the matter deliuered them vnto the Bassa his
master. Who therewith enraged, and calling her vnto him, forthwith
in his furie, with a dagger stabd her to the heart and slew her: so
togither with the death of his loue, hauing cured his tormenting
jealousie.[9]

The similarities between this story and that of Irene, even
to phrases almost identical, are obvious, and such as might
easily lead to a telescoping of the two in the memory. Thus
Irene, with Manto's involuntary assistance, could become
a much more vivid and sympathetic character.

The chief differentiating feature between the five Irenes
in question lies in their relationship to one or two other
persons. Knolles's Irene is, as we saw, a mere passive
instrument in Mahomet's hands. The reality of Swinhoe's
turns on her devotion to her husband, which conditions
her bearing toward Mahomet. The Irene of 1664 is
similarly devoted to her lover Justinianus, and cajoles
Mahomet for identical reasons. Neither of these women
is sufficiently alive to the charms of greatness to have to
face a real choice. Goring's Irene, already violated, is
almost solely conditioned by that fact. The motive of love
is no longer of vital importance to her, nor does it count

for much in the play as a whole. Johnson does nothing to restore the loss to her directly. But he makes amends by two innovations which we shall consider in due course.

A dramatist's problem with Irene is, as I have suggested, chiefly one of directing her allegiances, in order to secure the interest and sympathy of the audience. In this light, it is plain that she recedes in tragic interest, or at least in pathetic interest, with each successive play. Swinhoe's Irene, in dignity, in beauty, in passion and power to move, surpasses all her later avatars. The Irene of 1664 hardly calls on our pity before we become confident that in the end she will be happy. To be sure, we sympathize and are solicitous for her welfare, but our anxiety is not allowed to become acute. There is no trace of the tragic heroine in her. Goring's Irene, on the contrary, is intended to make a strong bid for the role of pathetic heroine, of the Nicholas Rowe *genre*. She somehow misses of due effect, perhaps because Goring lacks the creative force to make a passive character interesting. The worst has already happened to her; her story, but for the *coup de grâce*, was finished before the play began. She has only one topic, her own misery, and she is dull on that. Goring has retained her love for a lover; but it can do no work because neither she nor anyone else believes in its potency. Johnson's Irene has been still further robbed of the appeals of a tragic heroine. Her heart is disengaged; we are not called upon for tender solicitude on that score. Neither, by all his efforts, has Mahomet touched her affections by the end of the play any more deeply than just to bring her to a favourably receptive state of mind. In compensation, Johnson has supplied her with a new conflict; but it does not make up for what she has lost. The forces that struggle in her are Worldly Glory and allegiance to Christianity. The battle is obscure, and she has all but capitulated to

Glory when we first meet her. She does not convince us that religion has any purchase on her emotional life. Indeed, it hardly appears that she is capable of any profound emotion save the fear of death. The fall of Constantinople, with all the terrors of its siege and sack, has left scarcely a surface scratch on her consciousness. For her the world is still brave and new. But she is too vacillating and unimpassioned to impart much life to such an attitude. Actually, she is one of the least interesting characters in the play. Had she deeply loved Mahomet, and been heroically trying to save him from an assassin's dagger when he gave orders for her destruction . . . !

What, then, of Mahomet? It is obvious, looking at the *donnée* of the fable, that the moment the heroine is allowed to arouse a lively sympathy and interest, the problem of Mahomet's rôle becomes acute. Can his passionate devotion to a lovely and lovable woman be reconciled with his deliberate murder of her in the height of that emotion? Bandello thought not, and flatly denied that Mahomet was capable of love. Knolles, for whose purposes the general truth of Mahomet's character is essential, manages to convince by the fullness of his historical narrative and abundant characterization in other, easily credible, contexts, as well as by leaving Irene a mere symbolic cipher, standing for one of the forces which a statesman must overcome. He thus carries us through this disturbance by his own momentum, and ignores Bandello's disclaimer. But stage representation intensifies the difficulty; and Swinhoe, having failed to seize upon the only motive—jealousy—which would induce an unforced conviction, evidently does not dare the finale in its original melodramatic form. He creates instead a situation where death for Irene, at the hands of her declared enemies, is imminent and apparently inevitable; so that Mahomet's stroke, unpremeditated as it is, takes on the look of a mercy killing. Even then, Mahomet cannot strike the blow until Irene has already lost consciousness.

The anonymous author of 1664, as we have seen, cut the Gordian knot and made a happy ending. But Goring, reverting to the original outline, bolsters his solution in two ways. His Mahomet has learned the bitter mockery of his technical success over Irene; and he hears from her own lips that her heart is still in another man's possession. Thus, if he had no further motive than jealousy, his violence would be plausible. But this motive is synchronized with a strong appeal to his impulse to power, directed by three of his most trusted, respected friends. Much is made of his suffering on both these counts, before the coronation and stabbing of Irene. There is no doubt that Goring, however bad his play may be on other grounds, has solved the particular difficulty of Mahomet better than any of his predecessors, while yet keeping closest to the original climax.

Johnson gives a fresh solution, causing Mahomet to turn against Irene out of a belief that she intended treachery against him. In this case, Mahomet is credible —even, in some degree, sympathetic, because it is Abdalla who collects the chief odium of the catastrophe. Johnson thus avoids the psychological dilemma of Knolles in an equally convincing way.

Nichol Smith's remark, that the interest of these plays, for the reader of Johnson, lies almost wholly in the treatment of Irene, seems less and less true for each successive play. Nor does it appear by any means a safe assumption that Johnson had no acquaintance with the first two. We know that his father was a bookseller; and we know that Johnson as a youth read omnivorously. It is perfectly possible that Johnson ran across any or all of these plays among the quantities of odd literature that must have passed through his father's hands. It is not my primary object to argue specific indebtedness: I am concerned rather to see what illumination can be thrown upon Johnson's play by inspecting other dramatic renderings of the same basic materials. But it does appear, I believe, that several of the features that distinguish Johnson's rendition from that of Knolles had already been added to the story by the time it reached Johnson. These additions are most strikingly evident in the version of 1664. There we find —it may be as well to enumerate the parallels—a similar doubling, or dividing, of the romantic interest by the introduction of a new pair of lovers; similar friendships between the two men and between the women; transference of Mahomet's infatuation from a lesser light to Irene herself; the setting of both plays in the royal gardens; access in disguise, of the men to the ladies; the secret preparation of a vessel for escape; similar prominence given to Mustapha's disclosure to Mahomet of the Aga's (Cali's) treachery; similar transformation of Knolles's traitorous or cowardly Justinianus into an heroic figure; similar magnanimity from captor to captive, Janizary to Justinianus, Demetrius to Caraza; similar mollifying of the picture of Turkish severity. Finally, there is the introduction of an intellectual theme: Love *vs.* Honour in 1664, Glory *vs.* Religion in Johnson. A few of these elements appear, as we saw, in Swinhoe, or in Goring, or both, but not in such strong combination as in 1664.[10] Indeed, the noticeable weakness of the role of Leontius in Johnson's play could best be explained by assuming Johnson's ill-advised retention from 1664 of a character for whom he had little or no dramatic use. By eliminating a Leontius-Irene connection, Johnson robbed Leontius of his only vital function, so that we have left the spectacle of a leader of higher military standing entering the plot only to listen to Demetrius's and Cali's plans, and to lament that his own part—to get

the bark in readiness with its complement of patriots—
is merely

> To wait remote from Action, and from Honour,
> An idle List'ner to the distant Cries
> Of slaughter'd Infidels, and Clash of Swords!

He protests (iv, iii) against this ignoble rôle, but is immediately humbled by Demetrius's charge of selfishly preferring personal glory before his country's welfare. In the version of 1664, the corresponding figure had entered at an identical late moment in the plot, and after being offered leadership had magnanimously refused first place. But his real business in the play was to make up the foursome of lovers. Had Johnson preserved this function, it would have enlivened Irene as well as Leontius and the audience. But before we pass to the consideration of Johnson's reasons for making this change, it will be best to look at certain lesser matters.

Perhaps surprisingly, at the very time when Johnson was engaged on the composition of *Irene*, another dramatist across the Channel was working on the same theme. Composed at Strasbourg, the *Mahomet Second* of Jean Sauvé de la Noue was first acted in Paris on the 23rd of February, 1739. It was so successful as to hold the stage for more than a generation. Whether Johnson knew the play I cannot say. I suspect not; but, except his own, it is the only one of the lot in which Irene has no previous engagement, no former lover. And similarly, perhaps in consequence, La Noue's is the only other Irene besides Johnson's to feel persuasive force in the possibility of helping her people as an argument for accepting Mahomet: in both plays she is really won by this to accept his proposals. For the rest, there is little similarity. La Noue's Mahomet is psychologically unconvincing. At the opening he is all complaisance, all desire to ease the lot of the suffering Christians. Then, after his lust for fame is reawakened, he comes to Irene just as her charms have subdued her particular foes, and deliberately, when there is least reason, stabs her in their presence, partly because he feels that they do not deserve the happiness of having her as their Queen (!), and partly as a sacrifice to his own ambition: 'je l'immole à ma gloire'. This, roughly, is the position of Knolles's Mahomet, and it will hardly do on the stage.

Voltaire made La Noue's play the subject of a very interesting letter, in which he aired his unorthodox but characteristic views of the character of Mahomet. [Letter dated April 3, 1739: cf. *Works*, ed. of 1877, vol. XXXIII, pp. 236–241.] As we might guess, he reverses the traditional picture of the tyrant and the cruelties of his siege of Constantinople, repudiates the Irene story, presents Mahomet as a highly educated, enlightened monarch, and uses him and the Turks generally as sticks to beat the Christians. In the same years, Voltaire was working on his *Essai sur les Mœurs*, in which the ninety-first and ninety-second chapters develop the same ideas at greater length. [*Works*, 1877, vol. XII, pp. 98 ff.] The book was not published for some years, and Johnson may never have seen it.

Voltaire, though he may have given Garrick a notion or two in production, would anyhow never have affected Johnson. As for La Noue, it seems safe to conclude that he had no effect. Johnson's play was probably finished before he could have read or learned about La Noue's; and the first draft proves that the points in which there is a resemblance were present in the English play from the beginning. We may be confident that, during the decade in which Johnson's work was waiting for performance, he would neither have sought nor avoided an opportunity to become acquainted with the French play, and that he would not have revised his own in the light of it.

There would have been more likelihood of his getting to know Voltaire's Turkish play, for this, in an English version called *Mahomet the Impostor*, by James Miller, was produced at Drury Lane in 1744, with Garrick in the role of Zaphna. This play is not about the second Mahomet, but about the founder of the religion which bears his name. Save that Voltaire was familiar with the Irene legend and perhaps borrowed certain elements from it to fill up his own, parallels are doubtless purely fortuitous. Thus, old Alcanor, who in Voltaire's play corresponds roughly to Cali as leader of resistance to Mahomet, has charge of the captive Fair, and disclaims interest on account of his age:

> Smile not, my Friend, nor think that at these Years,
> Well travell'd in the Winter of my Days,
> I entertain a Thought tow'rds this young Beauty,
> But what's as pure as is the Western Gale....
>   This Heart, by Age and Grief congeal'd,
> Is no more sensible to Love's Endearments,
> Than are our barren Rocks to Morn's sweet Dew.

> [Miller's version, ed. of 1744, p. 4]

When Johnson's Mahomet gives Irene into the charge of old Cali, he says:

> Sure, chill'd with sixty winter Camps, thy Blood
> At Sight of female Charms will glow no more.

To which Cali replies:

> These Years, unconquer'd MAHOMET, demand
> Desires more pure, and other Cares than Love. [I, v, 5–8]

It is interesting that, in Johnson's first draft, Irene tentatively puts forward a plea for apostasy which is the converse of Alcanor's declaration of natural morality. Irene says: 'that the Supreme Being will accept of Virtue whatever outward circumstances it may be accompanied with, and may be delighted with Varieties of Worship. but is Answer'd That Variety cannot affect that being who infinitely happy in his own perfections wants no external gratifications, nor can infinite Truth be delighted with falsehood. that though he may guide or pity those he leaves in Darkness. he abandons those who shut their eyes against the beams of Day'. [Fol. 12.] Alcanor, in Voltaire, declares:

> Thou know'st but little, *Zaphna*,
> If thou dost think true Virtue is confin'd
> To Climes or Systems; no, it flows spontaneous,
> Like Life's warm Stream throughout the whole Creation,
> And beats the Pulse of ev'ry healthful Heart.
>   [Miller's version, p. 39 (III, i)]

Voltaire's play, of course, also sounds the note of apostasy. It is, again, a curious coincidence that Zaphna, who is in a position comparable to that of Johnson's Abdalla, as a tool to commit murder, is given a slow-working poison that just permits him to accomplish the act before he himself expires. For this is exactly Abdalla's plan, with Cali's connivance, to get rid of Demetrius, who is first to kill Mahomet. [*Irene*, IV, iv, 30–33.] In Voltaire's play, the poison prevents Zaphna from killing Mahomet's self; in Johnson's, it is dashed to the ground just before reaching Demetrius's lips.

I do not, I repeat, wish to press resemblances which may be quite accidental, into service as arguments for parenthood. It is enough to say that the plays at which we have been looking are part of the background of Johnson's *Irene*, and that there is no reason for concluding him to have been entirely ignorant of that background.

There is always a kind of magnetism at work in the literary world that, given time, tends to make us aware of what others have done with the same or related materials. In the present case, we know that Johnson, contrary to his later habit, even took the trouble to do some special reading in the field, aside from what he may casually have picked up in books or conversation.

II. THE FIRST DRAFT

The first draft of *Irene* is an extraordinary document, difficult to understand but containing very valuable hints for the student of Johnson's mind. The manuscript, as Boswell tells us in the *Life*, is in the King's Library (British Museum MS 306), having been bound with a transcript made by Bennet Langton and presented by him to the King. Johnson, 'a few days before his death', had picked out the draft from a mass of papers he was burning and had given it to Langton. It is written on both sides of twenty leaves measuring approximately six by eight inches, numbered, apparently by Johnson himself, by leaves consecutively, at the right-hand top corner of the recto. The pages are quite filled as far as to the top of 19^b. There are frequent marginalia and symbols of cross-reference on the left-hand margins. Since the pages are now separated and inlaid for safety, it is probably impossible to determine whether they formerly composed a slender notebook or not. But it is clear that Johnson proceeded inconsistently: sometimes the text is continued overleaf or from verso to following recto, sometimes from recto to recto, sometimes from verso to verso. But there are further irregularities. The matter on a single page is sometimes disconnected: thus, 9^b continues a third of the way down on page 10^b. The top third of 10^b is not carried on from 10^a (which continues on 11^a); and the lower half of 10^b is unconnected with what goes above. A synopsis of acts and scenes starts on 10^a, skips 10^b, continues on 11^a and 11^b; skips to 16^a - 16^b; then reverts to 6^a and finishes on 6^b. The likeliest reason for the skip from 11^b to 16^a is that the intervening pages were already filled. Pages 13^a to 15^a are continuously linked by speeches that run onto the following page. The top of 12^b is another try at a speech of Mahomet occurring previously at the top of 12^a; and the rest of 12^a and 12^b is mostly concerned with argument between Aspasia and Irene. 12^b and 13^a are not connected; but 12^a appears to continue 10^b. Since 11^a obviously continues 10^a, it must belong where it is. There is no title-page nor any title at all. Page one contains a descriptive list of characters, which is further elaborated on the verso of folio three. Intervening, from 1^b to the bottom of 3^a, are discontinuous parts of speeches in verse or prose, resumed towards the bottom of 3^b and continuing to the bottom of 5^b without interruption. At 6^a Johnson suddenly begins to outline. the content of Act V, going on to the bottom of 6^b, where he ends with the closing lines of the play. Folios 7 to 9 inclusive continue with disconnected speeches as before, and the procedure is resumed at 17^a and kept up to the top of 19^b.

When the manuscript was printed for the first time in full, in Nichol Smith's and McAdam's valuable edition of Johnson's *Poems*, Oxford, 1941, its contents were partially rearranged in the interests of clarity and ease of reading; and in the revised edition of the *Poems* in the Yale *Johnson*, 1964, the passages corresponding to the formerly printed text of the play are interpolated as footnotes for comparative reference. But without going to the original manuscript the student cannot tell exactly where the breaks occur at the page's end, and hence which pages run on continuously or fail to do so, so that the fragmentary eruption of Johnson's ideas is partially obscured in the editing.

Johnson's procedure, as it appears in this manuscript, is highly unusual and suggestive. For the most part, it consists of setting down completely unconnected passages, one after another, without any identification of speakers, and, as the final text proves, without any regard to the order of scenes intended. Either Johnson had his characters' roles so fully worked out in his mind before he began this draft that it was unnecessary for him to write down the attributions, or else he was as yet careless to fix the sentiments upon individuals. That he was not yet quite certain of his characters is proved by the list of persons on the first page, where several names are given of minor characters that do not appear in the play. It is also probably indicative, that he had almost filled the notebook before he decided to give Leontius his present name. Up to folio 17, Leontius is called Arsanes (from Knolles, whose Arsanes is a Corinthian prince married to the sister of Demetrius). Moreover, that there was in the draft no general working through the sequence of scenes appears from the fact that there is stuff for Act I as late as folio 18ᵃ, for Act II on 18ᵇ, and for Act III on 19ᵃ—the last full page of speeches in the manuscript.

The extraordinary economy—if one may so call it—or the unwillingness to write more than was necessary may be illustrated by two or three odd points. Near the top left-hand margin of the front page, Johnson set down in index fashion, one below the other, the figures 1 through 5, with an = sign after all but the first. This was intended for a table to guide him to the pages where the synopsis of each act occurred. He noted down the page reference for Act II—'2 = 11'—and left the other four acts unsupplied with their corresponding figures. The single reference, in actual fact, was virtually sufficient, because when he turned to it he would find the synopsis of Act I on the preceding leaf; of Act III, on the verso of folio 11, continued thence by reference to 16, where Act IV began. Act IV in turn continued overleaf, where began Act V, with a backward reference to its conclusion on folio 6. But what restraint! How could a man refrain from filling up that simple key, the incompleteness of which stared him in the face every time he took up the manuscript? Again, in his descriptive table of characters on the same page, he writes after Irene's name only thus much: 'A Grecian Lady belov'd by Mahomet who for a Crown &c.' The '&c' stands, of course, for Irene's willingness to become an apostate to the Christian faith. Once more, on folio 16, Johnson summarizes IV, IV thus: 'Mahomet calls upon them all to...joy for his Success with Irene whom he h. n. g. that tomorrow he will espouse her as Queen.' There seems no reason to contradict Langton's interpretation that the cryptic letters stand for 'has now gained', unless it be thought that some Latin phrase would be more likely to be so abridged. But his economy is displayed perhaps even more strikingly in the fact that, chaotic as was the state of the dialogue at this stage, there is virtually nothing, beyond two or three brief speeches, which does not find its counterpart, often in identical words, in the finished play. And conversely, though there is matter for every act, nearly a third of the scenes in the play find no single contributory line in the draft, while for nearly two-thirds there are fewer than a dozen lines apiece—most frequently fewer than six.

It can hardly be doubted, in view of the nature of the manuscript, that it is really the *first* draft of the play. Whatever preceded must have been written almost solely on the tables of memory. Nor will the supposition be difficult to accept in the light of what is elsewhere disclosed of his habits of composition. He told Boswell, it will be recalled, that he would make fifty or more verses at a time, walking up and down while he shaped them in his head, and writing down nothing until he had done the lot. Then, and then only, he would record them, frequently writing but half of each line, because of indolence; as knowing that the cues would call up the rest, or perhaps confident that if they failed he could produce as good or better with little additional effort. Seventy lines of *The Vanity of Human Wishes* he composed in this way in a morning, writing them down later. He could recall the exact phrasing of a letter after an interval of years. This first draft, then, probably contains all he troubled to set down up to that point. Moreover, his saving it and nothing else,[11] chaotic and awkward though it was, may be taken as a hint that there was nothing further to save until he sat down to write the play strictly through. For it seems unlikely that he would have clung to this manuscript, with all its handicaps as a working copy, if there had been convenient to his use, instead, a preliminary or intermediate draft of the scenes in their approximate order. In view of Johnson's habits and powers, it is not improbable that the next draft was the manuscript of the whole play in its roughly final form, with such interlineations and corrections as might thereafter occur. After that, a clean copy of the completed drama, to submit to Fleetwood and others. 'Keep Irene close', he wrote to John Taylor in 1742: at that time there was perhaps but the one perfect copy in existence.

But the first draft contains other, more valuable revelations of his creative techniques and of the scenes with which he was first and most intensely preoccupied. By his habit, in the draft, of reverting again and again to certain episodes, he demonstrates beyond contradiction that his own interest in the play focused overwhelmingly upon two points. Neither of them, in the terms in which he was thinking, was inherently dramatic. First in importance was the argument against apostasy; next was the cause of the sudden downfall of Constantinople. After these, and at some distance, come two other cluster-points to which he several times reverted, the first being Mahomet's wooing—if that could so be called which wooing was none—and the second, Cali's unsuccessful attempt to get leave from Mahomet for his pretended pilgrimage.

In the detached speeches or scraps of speeches of which the draft is largely composed, there is, from start to finish, hardly a single block of consecutive conversation. The nearest approaches are in brief prose hints of arguments on two sides of a question. As, for example, thus:

When Arsanes wonders that Heav'n should suffer the impious Cause to prevail—Demetr. answers that Man suffers not Heav'n by the Loss of his Temples and [altars] ill-defended, that The justice of Heav'n is honourd by ruin as the Mercy by preservation. That Worlds combine in the praises of their Maker. That bad men with the instructions of true Religion, are worse tha[n] Bad men with a worse Religion. Vices will have their effect   then particularises the faults that brought on the Greek fall. [Fol. 9ᵇ.]

It is noteworthy that in all such passages Johnson has committed his weight to one side, and thinks of settling the argument rather than of creating the impression of inconclusive conversational give-and-take. A very large part of the draft, in fact, looks like a statement of points for debate, without any sort of structural frame. What is not of this kind is generally either elegant descriptive phrase or aphoristic generalization such as: 'wherever Fear can fly revenge can follow'.

There could hardly be a clearer demonstration than this manuscript of what seems to us the radically untheatrical quality of Johnson's imagination. Out of such materials no living dialogue could rise. The draft is more a commonplace-book than a dramatic sketch. It is the record of a mind pondering certain chosen topics—not, one would guess, at all continuously, but intermittently recurring to them, concerned to set down any good idea or phrase that might rise into consciousness. When a new hint springs to mind, down it goes in the next vacant space, and a marginal reference from the last kindred occurrence points the way to the new entry farther along. Thus we can run a thread through the maze of disjunct elements, when we wish to string together those of a kind. The practice is more saving of paper than if Johnson had sorted as he went, and entered similar or related speeches on separate sheets.

This mode of composition makes clearer why there is so little real measuring of hostile points of view against each other in the finished scenes. We could not expect from it any of that wrestling of personalities which, meeting in unforeseen ways, reveals character in the Shakespearean dialogue. Such a scene as that between Claudio and Isabella, where unsuspected facets of character currently flash out under the twisting pressures of argument, is unthinkable in the commonplace-book. But, short of this, we might have looked in Johnson, a resourceful master of debate, for a sinewy and realistic grappling of points of view, where the successive stages rise immediately out of their opposing positions. That, too, would be essential intellectual drama, if not necessarily good theatre. But neither is such a result forthcoming from the commonplace-book technique. The separate speeches are sterilized from vital contact with their fellows. The individual gems are wrapped in cotton, not allowed to touch. Dryden, in his heroic plays, with something of a kindred notion of lofty artificiality of diction, yet contrived to strike one stone against another, even though each glitters distinct. The two minds had a similar intellectual athleticism and power of illustrative invention; but the younger man failed to profit by that great example. That Johnson's play is dramatically as convincing as it is must be credited to the fact that the draft is no fuller; as, conversely, we can hold the draft to blame for much of the failure of the finished work really to fuse. For, had he first written off whole scenes as natural dialogue, trusting to extemporaneous invention for filling the mould, and then perhaps enriching, his native power as exhibited in his own conversation must have come more conspicuously into play. Instead, he was constantly dredging up another nugget out of the lode, stopping the flow of argument to fix it in place.

Unsatisfying as the dialogue is in debate, it is in the statement of emotion that it most disappoints. Too visible is a kind of third-person habit of mind that masquerades as a first-person statement, so that we get not the expression of feeling but the description of it. Thus, when Leontius mentions the probable fate of Aspasia, Demetrius cries out:

> Dear hapless Maid—*tempestuous Grief o'erbears*
> *My reasoning Pow'rs*—Dear, hapless, lost ASPASIA!

That is description of emotion, and the man that can speak it proves the opposite of what he says: his intellect is not overwhelmed with grief, but is noting such a condition as if in another person. How different in kind such a statement from the intimacy of an emotion which first keeps a stunned and anguished silence, and only when prodded says simply:

> I cannot but remember such things were
> That were most precious to me.

In contrast, Johnson here trusts neither himself nor the actor nor his audience, but yields to a compulsion to describe, with his eye turned not upon the object of primary solicitude, but upon a spectacle. The passage continues:

LEONTIUS. Suspend the Thought.
DEMETRIUS.　　　　　　　All Thought on her is Madness:
Yet let me think—I see the helpless Maid,
Behold the Monsters gaze with savage Rapture,
Behold how Lust and Rapine struggle round her.

That is not the way an anxious lover declares he cannot bear to think of what his love may be suffering. The ill lies deeper than a mere outmoded fashion in diction: it lies in a failure in imaginative insight, which has not been able to meet its final responsibility but has stopped short at the third-person, or narrative, stage. For diction may be of the last degree of artificiality, so it figure a genuine, present state of mind; as when, in the superb fourth act of Dryden's *Aureng-zebe*, Indamora moves through a kaleidoscopic shifting of emotional attitude towards her lover—from happiness to amazement, to incredulity, to pity, to indignation, to proud disdain, to indifference, to gentle forgiveness, to passionate acceptance. The series terminates in the following words:

> INDAMORA. Be no more jealous!
> AURENG-ZEBE. Give me cause no more:
> The danger's greater after, than before;
> If I relapse, to cure my jealousy,
> Let me (for that's the easiest parting) die.
> INDAMORA. My life!
> AURENG-ZEBE. My soul!
> INDAMORA. My all that Heavn can give!
> Death's life with you; without you, death to live.

These words come as the emotionally convincing conclusion of a scene to which one has no difficulty in granting the necessary suspension of disbelief.

To the difficult question 'What then is true expression of emotion?' I fear that in this place we may not stay for an answer; but we may safely assert that it will not have been approached until the chasm between third and first person has been crossed. In general, one may suspect that the eighteenth century was all too frequently blind to the chasm, possibly because of its faith in the power of description. Few ages, perhaps, have been so greatly preoccupied with emotion as an object to be contemplated, analysed, and described.[12] But, again perhaps, for that very reason it was the more easily misled into mistaking emotion described for emotion experienced.

It was said a moment ago that Johnson did not trust the actor. That this is a fact seems clear from the surface of his play. In all the important scenes, the scenes which have been laboured with the greatest care, there is nothing for an actor to do but, so to put it, to follow the directions on the bottle, to answer (if possible!) to the description supplied. Two examples will suffice. At her first and all-unexpected meeting with Demetrius, Aspasia is overcome with joy. Demetrius catalogues the symptoms:

> Why does the Blood forsake thy lovely Cheek?
> Why shoots this Chilness through thy shaking Nerves?
> Why does thy Soul retire into herself?

Here, at least, the actress is instructed what she must simulate. But when Demetrius first brings Leontius to meet Cali, the following dialogue takes place—and what is Leontius to be doing the while?—

> CALI. But can thy Friend sustain the glorious Cause...?
> DEMETRIUS. Observe him closely with a Statesman's Eye...
> CALI. His Mien is lofty, his Demeanour great,
> Nor sprightly Folly wantons in his Air,
> Nor dull Serenity becalms his Eyes.
> Such had I trusted once as soon as seen,
> But cautious Age suspects the flatt'ring Form,
> And only credits what Experience tells.
> Has Silence press'd her Seal upon his Lips?
> Does adamantine Faith invest his Heart?

And so on, through lines which ask whether, tried by a Tyrant's Frown, Ambition's Fire, a Friend's Embrace, or a Woman's Tears, he may not, respectively, bend, melt, soften, or flow dissolving.

Leontius has perhaps deserved the ordeal by the insensitive way in which he has just raised with Demetrius the question of Aspasia's unknown fate. Under the shelter of darkness, he says, he has roamed the streets of the desolated city:

> From ev'ry Palace burst a mingled Clamour,
> The dreadful Dissonance of barb'rous Triumph,
> Shrieks of Affright, and Wailings of Distress.
> Oft when the Cries of violated Beauty
> Arose to Heav'n, and pierc'd my bleeding Breast,
> I felt thy Pains, and trembled for Aspasia.

But at Demetrius's quick-answering agony, Leontius urges him to 'suspend the thought'.

We did not gather, however, for a field day at Johnson's expense. Such critical strictures resemble (at a great distance) his own objections to *Lycidas* in that on their own ground they are largely unanswerable, and that the ground in the main is uncontested. Only as they indicate the preoccupation of the author and his age do such ineptitudes—as these appear to us—claim critical notice.

III. THE PRIVATE CONTENT

We have now already made our way through the evidence of the draft back to the published text of *Irene*. In the light of both, and what we have learned of previous handlings of the story, we have yet to push our inquiry a little farther, if possible, into Johnson's special preoccupations. Can we, that is to say, use the play for any biographical illumination? Evidence of this kind is notoriously untrustworthy, but so much is known about Johnson, to control speculation, that it seems fairly safe to hazard a few deductions.

It is clear from the hints in Boswell and elsewhere that Johnson went through a youth of terrific storm and stress. As we have already observed, his inner condition during the years of early manhood was always barely below the point of eruption. Such, in fact, was the turmoil that it nearly cost him—he believed at one time that it was costing—his sanity. It manifested itself in instinctive opposition to authority of every kind—parental, pedagogical, social, political, theological. It resisted any sort of condescension or gesture of helpfulness. Johnson spurned the shoes that were left at his door in college, as he had beaten his schoolmistress in infancy for her anxiety to protect him. He did not want gifts: he wanted to wrest his rights. In after years, he vividly recalled this unruly turbulence. 'Ah, Sir', he said to Boswell of his college years, 'I was mad and violent....I was miserably poor, and I thought to fight my way by my literature and my wit; so I disregarded all power and all authority.'[13] 'To fire at all the established wits...to vanquish the great ones', he told Fanny Burney, had been his youthful delight.

Boswell himself speaks of 'that impetuosity of temper which never forsook' Johnson, and the fact is not in dispute. But the eight or ten years which preceded the composition of *Irene* must in many ways have been the most difficult years of his life. Everything in him was in ferment. His poverty, under the conditions of that time and place, was necessarily a matter of profound concern, forcing fundamental consideration of the structure of society. His father died in that period, and Johnson, upon receiving the £20 which was his from the effects, wrote in his diary: 'Usque adeo mihi fortuna fingenda est. Interea, ne paupertate vires animi languescant, nec in flagitia egestas abigat, cavendum'—which Boswell all too mildly translates, 'I now therefore see that I must make my own fortune. Meanwhile, let me take care that the powers of my mind may not be debilitated by poverty, and that indigence do not force me into any criminal act.'[14] Certain only of great abilities, he was entirely uncertain how to use them. He went through a miserable and humiliating experience as usher in Market-Bosworth school; and doubtless suffered as much or more in those other periods of vacancy, either at home or under his friend Hector's roof. The senses were clamouring for knowledge of life which he was as yet denying them. The whole problem of his religious convictions had to be fought through. Then, finally, still in his twenty-fifth year, and with his future course in life all undetermined, he married a widow in her middle forties—and began to labour at *Irene*. There is the emotional background of the play, and it is not unreasonable to look in it for some reflection of what he has come through.

It is fairly obvious that Johnson has but a perfunctory interest in the nominal heroine. As a character, she neither arouses his sympathy nor attracts his imagination. He is not concerned to realize and depict convincingly the wrestlings of this 'limèd soul', nor does he much care what becomes of her. Moreover, in contrast to his usual descriptive habit, he devotes little effort to suggesting her personal charms, beyond the general admission that she is beautiful and soft. She has no heart; she has never fallen in love. Her favouring Mahomet is portrayed as mere self-interest, and is so recognized even by Mahomet himself: he calls her base, and at the very moment of success despises her, and himself for doting on her. Only momentarily does she achieve solidity enough to cast a shadow, as when she taunts Aspasia with melancholy (v, ii), or anticipates her dignities just before the catastrophe (v, viii).

It is equally clear that Johnson has hardly more interest in Mahomet. Mahomet dotes, he threatens, he storms— and all is said. His psychological make-up is generalized to the vanishing point, and he already thinks so meanly of Irene that suspicion of her treachery could almost have presented itself as a welcome excuse for ridding him of an infatuation which has no grip on his essential being.

Nor does his fondness appear in conflict with the central drives of the empire builder: he intends a great new campaign to celebrate his marriage; he will 'conquer with Irene'.

The obvious dramatic interest in Mahomet lies potentially in this central conflict between irreconcilable compulsions, and his violent solution of it. The obvious dramatic interest of Irene lies potentially in an inner struggle, between either love and religion, or love and glory, or between glory and religion. Johnson wilfully discards the conflict in Mahomet; he excludes the love interest of Irene; and the Glory vs. Religion conflict goes almost by default. Why, then, did he choose this story?

The answer must be that, though Mahomet's concerns were a matter of indifference to Johnson, the problem of Irene—not Irene herself—was of importance to him. But it was most important that it should be clearly decided, not that the wrong side should be made vivid and alluring. If the perverse psychology of the heroine were not to be the focus of interest, the terms of the debate would have to be. But in the latter case, dramatic interest depends upon a relative equivalence of appeal. On the contrary, what Johnson had to say as forcefully as possible was that no such equivalence existed, that the attractions of one side were of no real weight. No one must be allowed to think it uncertain where the right decision lay, or that Irene lacked the ability to make it, or that she deserved to be sympathized with, or even much to be pitied, for failing to do so. The dilemma is patent: the exigencies of the dramatist are irreconcilable with the requirements of the Christian moralist.

It might be argued that Johnson's orthodoxy made him blind to the opposing appeal. But it would be truer, I believe, to say that his will to unshakable faith combined with his fear of losing what faith he had to make it

impossible for him to present a plausibly dramatic case for
the opposition. The violence which appears in him whenever the subject is raised is a notable feature of Boswell's
record. The questioning voice must be roared down. But
Johnson was a questioner by native endowment. The voice
was in himself. 'Everything', he once told Boswell,
'which Hume has advanced against Christianity had
passed through my mind long before he wrote.' It was
a terror to him that the intellect which ordinarily served
him so superbly had never been able in this all-important
matter to provide convincing answers to the questions.
The answer upon which he comes to anchor is not an
appeal to intellectual conviction, but an appeal to the
general consensus as opposed to individual fallibility. 'A
system, built upon the discoveries of a great many minds',
he declares, 'is always of more strength, than what is
produced by the mere workings of any one mind.... As
to the Christian religion, Sir, besides the strong evidence
which we have for it, there is a balance in its favour from
the number of great men who have been convinced of its
truth.'[15] But to believe beyond the limits of demonstration
ran counter to his basic instincts. The faith that he had
gave him little peace; and it was grounded in fear. 'None',
he once wrote, 'would have recourse to an invisible power,
but that all other subjects have eluded their hopes.'[16] He
blamed a sermon of Blair's for the statement that 'he who
does not feel joy in religion is far from the kingdom of
heaven'. 'There are many good men', he protested, 'whose
fear of God predominates over their love. It may discourage. It was rashly said.'[17] Hence, it is no surprise
that in the play *Irene* an exposition of the Christian point
of view that is intended to exhibit Irene's folly in the
strongest colours says nothing whatever about the love of
God, or the joys of religion, but is based almost entirely
on an appeal to fear. The opposition lies between the

absence of a negative—freedom from guilty self-reproach
—and the awful despair of the apostate 'beneath each
Curse of unrelenting Heav'n' [III, viii, 86].

One can hardly doubt, in face of the evidence of the
first draft, that the primary reason for Johnson's choosing
the story was that it gave him the opportunity to ad-
minister the instruction preached by Aspasia to Irene in
Act III, scene 8, and worked out in the *dénouement*. The
first tentative lines of the draft are upon this topic, and
Johnson recurs to it much more frequently throughout the
draft than to any other part of the play. Out of more than
two dozen trial passages for the scene, moreover, it is
significant that all but three or four are for the lesson itself.
He is not thinking of replies for Irene. As it took final
shape, the instruction is roughly as follows:

Giving up your religion for worldly ambition will make
it impossible for you even to be a true friend. You cannot
keep what virtue you will: the great sin will corrupt your
whole nature and you will be left to sink into total ruin.
Do not plead the fear of death as an excuse for yielding:
life and death are 'only varied modes' of eternal existence,
and life should be given up to preserve virtue. For the
end of life is virtue. We reasonably give up a lesser for
a greater good:

> Thus Life, with loss of Wealth, is well preserv'd,
> And Virtue cheaply sav'd with loss of Life.

Do not argue the good you could do with all this power:
the good intention does not justify the evil means. To
believe that it does so is to 'bid success become the test
of truth', to justify usurpation, bigotry, massacre, per-
secution, and every kind of excess. You will find, when
you have gained your desire, that your soul will stagnate
in sloth and you will not discover those opportunities
for doing good that you now anticipate. Yet you will have

no peace of mind, because of your gnawing guilt. Granted that ambition may argue a certain greatness of spirit: it is not power that is condemned, but 'power obtained by crime'. And nothing will assuage the apostate's pangs.

Such is the doctrine which is driven home with terrifying swiftness by Irene's fate. It is linked with another lesson enforced by Mustapha at the end of the play. In the draft, that lesson takes the following form:

> Man...by vice or passion driv'n
> Is but the executioner of Heavn
> When erring Fury throws the random dart
> Heav'n turns its point upon the guilty Heart
> Behold Irene—oe'rthrown
> By crimes abhord, and treasons not her own
> Eternal justice thus her doom decreed
> And in the traytress bad th'Apostate bleed.

But evidently Johnson saw the dangerous implications of this statement. It comes perilously near to justifying vice and passion as the chosen instruments of heaven's working-out of justice. Do, then, the righteous ends sanctify the evil means? The passage was revised into a much safer form:

> So sure the Fall of Greatness rais'd on Crimes,
> So fix'd the Justice of all-conscious Heav'n.
> When haughty Guilt exults with impious Joy,
> Mistake shall blast, or Accident destroy;
> Weak Man with erring Rage may throw the Dart,
> But Heav'n shall guide it to the guilty Heart.

Demetrius earlier had made the careful distinction in justifying to Aspasia his part in Cali's conspiracy. When she deplores the guilt which, intermixed, pollutes the good cause, Demetrius replies:

> Permitted oft, though not inspir'd by Heav'n,
> Successful Treasons punish impious Kings.

In his care, however, to dissociate heaven from the evil means of which it makes constant use, Johnson does not avoid another implication: namely, that heaven is incorrigibly opportunistic in executing its judgments by the most convenient means, be those means wicked or erring or merely inappropriate.

Had Johnson left Irene subject to the powerful appeal of love, he could not have settled the issues with such distinctness. Had she known a guilty love, she would have seemed to be punished for the sexual sin. Or, had she been restrained by love of—let us say—Leontius, there would have been little room left for piety to earn credit. For, had she enjoyed a commendable love, either she must have remained faithful, in which case the whole interest in her would have been deflected into sympathetic concern on that score; or she must have deserted her lover for power, in which case her falsehood to God and to man would have appeared to be equated, and she would be condemned by an audience more for the less serious offence than for her apostasy. If he was to make anything noteworthy of the religious message, therefore, Johnson had to detach Irene from the factor that had always made her interesting.

But he was not indifferent to the interest of love. Besides the consideration that a play lacking it could hardly succeed on the stage, he had in these early days of his marriage things he wanted to say about it, an attitude to get expressed. He saw his opportunity in the rôle of the confidante: she could be provided with a lover, and be endowed with whatever qualities the author chose, unhampered by Irene's special restrictions. In this development, as we saw, he had been anticipated by the Restoration playwright; but for Johnson there was a real necessity, and he so far extended the functions and importance of the confidante that she dominates the play. Almost all the interesting and attractive attributes which Irene had hitherto enjoyed are now subtracted from her and added to Aspasia. Not merely personal beauty and all the love interest of the play are Aspasia's, but religious fervour and intellectual power as well. She is more completely Johnson's own creation than any other of his characters. She is, in fact, his ideal woman, and as such she deserves our particular notice. She is, in the first place, remarkably beautiful and attractive to very different types of men. Besides the intellectual Demetrius, she had for a time subdued the sensual Mahomet, and the fire-eating Abdalla falls at her feet at the first glance. She has, in the second place, a piety secure from attack, and strong enough to govern all her attitudes, but of a sombre cast. The third notable characteristic is her masculine intellect, supported by masculine learning: a lady, says the draft, 'bred up in all the Learning of Greece'. Herein she acknowledges her debt to Demetrius. She wields her intellectual weapons with true Johnsonian vigour. Irene praises her for her 'Soul by Nature great, enlarg'd by Knowledge'; for her steady courage which braves the shocks of Fate; and hits off the whole character in a phrase certainly intended by Johnson as the highest compliment: 'all Aspasia but her Beauty's Man'. She had no tolerance of feminine timidity:

> The weakness we lament, our selves create,
> Instructed from our infant Years to court
> With counterfeited Fears the Aid of Man;
> We learn to shudder at the rustling Breeze,
> Start at the Light, and tremble in the Dark;
> Till Affectation, rip'ning to Belief,
> And Folly, frighted at her own Chimeras,
> Habitual Cowardice usurps the Soul.   [II, i, 26 ff.]

The feminine virtue which she upholds, however, in the face of physical dangers is 'passive Fortitude', not an Amazonian ideal. She confesses to real fears in the face of real perils. Withal, she is not ambitious for worldly distinctions. When Demetrius asks her how she will support the 'woes of exile', she is ready.

Nor wealth, nor Titles, make ASPASIA's Bliss....
Chearful I follow to the rural Cell,
Love be my Wealth, and my Distinction Virtue.

[IV, i, 106, 110–111]

Demetrius is her male counterpart, 'a Greek Nobleman versed in Philosophy and Literature'—again an ideal of the author. (How purely gratuitous the telltale endowment of 'Literature', an attribute which finds no opportunity to work in the play!) Each admires the other for the possession of enduring values, intellectual and spiritual; and each pays the other the final compliment:

> DEMETRIUS. Thou kind Assistant of my better Angel,
> Propitious Guide of my bewilder'd Soul,
> Calm of my Cares, and Guardian of my Virtue.
> ASPASIA. My Soul first kindled by thy bright Example,
> To noble Thought and gen'rous Emulation,
> Now but reflects those Beams that flow'd from thee.

[IV, i, 10–15]

Without insisting that Aspasia is a lover's portrait of Elizabeth Porter, one may yet feel quite certain that she is the essential embodiment of the qualities Johnson found, or tried to see, in the woman he married. In a true sense, this is Johnson's marriage offering. And one feels that in the main she deserved the tribute. Johnson, at twenty-five, overburdened with doubts and disadvantages and gloomy prospects, would have impressed most women of whatever age as a forbidding liability. His appearance, Lucy Porter told Boswell, was at that time 'very formidable'. One can hardly question the truth of her report. Scarred with scrofula, 'lean and lank', his 'immense structure of bones hideously striking', given to 'convulsive starts and odd gesticulations', and with anfractuosities of temper, the surprise and ridicule which Boswell says he tended to excite must, we may well suppose, have been among the least disagreeable of the emotions he would rouse in girls of his own age. How could he hope to find a wife until

the passage of years should have elicited public recognition of his merit? On the contrary, Elizabeth Porter made
him the supreme gift of her immediate belief and confidence in him, unmistakably and finally, at a time when
it was all-important to him to be possessed of such faith.
In a woman still in vigorous maturity, not unattractive in
appearance—her picture, Mrs Thrale said, was 'very
pretty' (better testimony than that of the mischievous
Garrick, embroidering his schoolboy recollections),—
possessed as well of modest means: the difference in years,
grotesque in the eyes of the world, must have been the
ultimate and reassuring flattery to Johnson, establishing
and confirming his sense of his own worth. 'Flaring and
fantastick in her dress' she may have been—Johnson at
that time would scarcely have been able to judge; but that
she was 'affected both in her speech and general behaviour' is hard to believe. She must, as Boswell says,
'have had a superiority of understanding and talents'; for
what she discerned and valued in her suitor was sterling.
'This', she told her daughter, 'is the most sensible man
that I ever saw in my life.' There is no reason to suppose
that Johnson was more deceived in her essential qualities
than she was in his. In her he found the response he
needed, and 'she certainly [to quote Boswell once more]
inspired him with a more than ordinary passion'.[18]

Sense is a virtue that is found in abundance in Aspasia,
as it is in Demetrius. Nor is it impossibly fanciful to
overhear Johnson's feeling toward his wife in Demetrius's
address:

> Propitious Guide of my bewilder'd Soul,
> Calm of my Cares, and Guardian of my Virtues.

For this is literally what she was to him at that time. The
reading is confirmed, moreover, by the fact that the
women to whom in later life Johnson was most strongly

attracted were approximations to the Aspasian ideal: women of pronounced intellectual development, fond of rational discussion, literary, 'unlike the trifling Race of vulgar Beauties' (*Irene*, IV, i, 18), yet unmistakably womanly.

In one other note that sounds not infrequently through the play it is possible to hear overtones of the author's immediate experience. Away from home, in unfriendly London, it would not be surprising if the thought of separation struck Johnson with peculiar force. There seems to be a personal reverberation when the idea recurs, whether to Demetrius, or to Aspasia, or even to Mahomet. We hear it when Demetrius refers to 'this age of absence' which has separated him from Aspasia; and in Aspasia's prayer:

> Soon may we meet again, secure and free,
> To feel no more the Pangs of Separation.
>
> [IV, ii, 23–24; also III, x, 39]

We hear it perhaps even more loudly, because here it is less natural to the context, in Mahomet's complaint:

> Why rove I now, when absent from my Fair,
> From Solitude to Crouds, from Crouds to Solitude,
> Still restless, till I clasp the lovely Maid,
> And ease my loaded Soul upon her Bosom?
>
> [I, iv, 9 ff.]

It is noteworthy that there is no appearance of the idea of separation in the first draft—a fact which, were there other evidence to support the conjecture, might lead to the conclusion that the play was planned and carried through the rough stage in the country, but brought to completion in London in a much more thoroughgoing sense than is generally supposed.[19]

As a final commentary on what has been said of this aspect of his play, I cannot forbear to quote part of the letter to his wife of January 31, 1739/40,[20] called by Birkbeck Hill 'the gem of my collection':

Dearest Tetty,

After hearing that you are in so much danger,... I shall be very uneasy till I know that you are recovered, and beg that you will omit nothing that can contribute to it.... You have already suffered more than I can bear to reflect upon, and I hope more than either of us shall suffer again. One part at least I have often flatterd myself we shall avoid for the future, our troubles will surely never separate us more.... I still promise myself many happy years from your tenderness and affection, which I sometimes hope our misfortunes have not yet deprived me of. David [Garrick] wrote to me this day on the affair of Irene, who is at last become a kind of Favourite among the Players.... I hope it will at length reward me for my perplexities....

Be assured, my dear Girl, that I have seen nobody in these rambles upon which I have been forced, that has not contribute[d] to confirm my esteem and affection for thee, though that esteem and affection only contributed to encrease my unhappiness when I reflected that the most amiable woman in the world was exposed by my means to miseries which I could not relieve.

I am

My charming Love

Yours

SAM: JOHNSON.

IV. THE ARTIFACT

Most readers of to-day come to *Irene* because of a previous interest in its author, and a single reading allays their curiosity about the play forever. Certainly, the reflection of Johnson's personality and view of life is for us the source of the keenest and most spontaneous, as well as most abiding, interest in it. This is equally true whether the expression of the man behind the words is merely implicit or comparatively outspoken. It vivifies, for example, our reading of Demetrius's analysis of the fall of Constantinople (or 'Greece') to make the application to England that was in Johnson's mind at the time. Of course, it was a proven fact, demonstrated in a dozen cases in recent dramatic history, that there was no quicker way to win a hearing than to inject a modicum of contemporary politics into a play by transparent allusion. But Johnson's other writings of the same period—his *London, Marmor Norfolciense*, and the ironic *Vindication of the Licensers*—make it evident that in him it was no display of *ad hoc* patriotic rant to denounce the avarice, vice, and self-interest that he saw rampant in the government of the late 'thirties. At this time he was a 'patriot'—that is, an enemy to Walpole—and there is plenty of conviction in his jeremiad against

> A feeble Government, eluded Laws,
> A factious Populace, luxurious Nobles,
> And all the Maladies of sinking States.

The contrasted ideal, the England of his dream, is depicted, of course, in Cali's later speech:

> If there be any Land, as Fame reports,
> Where common Laws restrain the Prince and Subject,
> A happy Land, where circulating Pow'r
> Flows through each Member of th'embodied State,
> Sure, not unconscious of the mighty Blessing,
> Her grateful Sons shine bright with ev'ry Virtue;
> Untainted with the Lust of Innovation,
> Sure all unite to hold her League of Rule
> Unbroken as the sacred Chain of Nature,
> That links the jarring Elements in Peace.   [1, ii, 55 ff.]

On the whole, I believe it to be true that much of the pleasure which a reader may experience in the play lies in spying through chinks of this sort; and even in what amounts to a sort of unmaking, a reversal of the processes that went to its construction. It would be possible to stop there; but such a dissolution is, rightly regarded, not the proper end of critical analysis. We wish to destroy the work in order to commence with the author its reconstitution, divining as best we may the choices that lay open to him as he went along, and estimating the final result in the light of a sympathetic understanding. We may be more interested in Johnson than in his play; but his synthesis is, temporarily at least, the culminating point of our concern with the man; and we should end, as we began, with the completed artifact. In its way, the *Irene* is a sort of diploma of Johnson's intellectual, emotional, and aesthetic maturity.

Some of his more private needs in writing his play have already been touched upon. We have seen that personal preoccupations with religion and love, reaching a point of tentative resolution in recent experience, made some kind of utterance almost necessary. But neither by temperament nor by time could Johnson nakedly obtrude his private history on the public notice. The day of intimate confessions would arrive half a century later. Meantime, the dignified solution was to subsume the particular under some sort of generalized dramatic projection. We have to consider what were the special satisfactions of this kind of release.

The evidence of the first draft hints at the care with which Johnson worked up the background of his play. He read and reread Knolles, took note, even with page references, of various details: of the artistic taste and the learning of Mahomet; of the method by which, during the night, he got his fleet over the isthmus to the inner harbour, so as to attack Constantinople where defence was least prepared; of the name of his admiral in the subsequent engagement. He went to De Herbelot's Oriental Encyclopædia for information about Mohammedan notions of the next world, of their ritualistic practices and their shrines. He looked out the vivid descriptions of Constantinople in Sandys's Journey, with its finely engraved plates depicting the mosqued and minareted city. Obviously, his mind was full of atmosphere and local colour when he commenced to write. And he fixed the scene as 'a Garden near the Walls of Constantinople'; the time as ten days after the city's fall. He had in mind also Knolles's picture of the city as the wealthy and splendid seat of the Eastern Empire under Constantinus Palaeologus.

All these details must have been required for the due operation of Johnson's creative imagination. Yet it is startling to watch their evaporation as he proceeds. A reference to 'Sophia's Temple', and one to 'tow'ring Domes' and 'shatter'd Spires', are all that finally remain to distinguish the Byzantine capital. Even from the stage directions its name disappears. Its polyglot and heterogeneous character is simplified to a suggestion of unified nationality, even to a city-state, regularly referred to as 'Greece', with which are associated the ideals of patriotism and liberty. The time is blurred to an indistinct period at which the conquerors have tired of destruction and pillage; the scene is no longer identified. In place of the details of Mohammedan culture, the barest references to Mecca, the Seraglio, belief in the Houris and the soullessness of women, suffice. Allusions to cannon and to 'mines discovered' are almost all that is left of that siege which Knolles earlier, and Gibbon later, chronicled with such impressive particularity. Neither the Turkish admiral nor the miraculous transporting of the fleet appears; nor is Mahomet permitted to display his science or his literature. It would seem, indeed, that all that groundwork of detail was prerequisite only that Johnson might push up his generalizations from firmer roots. He must have numbered the streaks of the tulip before he can remark general properties and large appearances. Before he neglects the minuter discriminations, he must have observed them with some attention. Only so will he fix upon the prominent and striking features. This is an aspect of neoclassical procedure seldom remarked. In truth, the method may be thought of as a kind of shorthand, which every lively intelligence can be left to develop at pleasure. Resourceful minds like Johnson's, in any case, will supply a rich context to generalization from their own stores; and feel a kind of impatience when everything is done for them.

The Prologue makes the claim that the play exhibits Nature 'ennobled, yet unchang'd'; that neither are the heroes gods, nor the lovers fools. Herein, that is to say, we are notified of a return from the heroic drama of recent years to a saner pattern, consonant with 'Reason, Nature, Truth'. The cloudland of the heroic play was never a country in which Johnson cared to dwell. Years later, he was to write: 'He that forsakes the probable may always find the marvellous.' And there is no profit in finding the marvellous, because 'we are affected only as we believe'.

What we believe is what we know and recognize. So that, at one extreme, following this doctrine plunges us finally into naturalism, a method that gets its purchase on our acceptance by the incessant cataloguing of familiar objects, and by the portrayal of a humanity drenched and conditioned by such things. At first glance no two things could be farther apart than characteristic artifacts of the neoclassical and the naturalistic schools. Yet they converge upon similar goals, and their means are curiously complementary. Both of them aim at the norm of human nature, and reject the idiosyncratic and inexplicable. Both therefore deal with the typical, the one because controlled by the belief that the greatest value and use lie there, the other because exceptions do not convincingly illustrate the pressure of basic and widespread forces. But, whereas the naturalist attempts definition by packing the environment into as solid a mould as possible for the object to be infused—or interred, so the other cuts away everything extraneous in order to expose the essential object with the least possible obstruction of contour. Latterly, there have been abundant signs of surfeit upon the indigestible banquet of sense data which the fiction, especially, of the last half-century or more has provided. It may therefore be an opportune moment to explore again that older method of pursuing essential reality. Sick of over-eating, let us meditate the benefits of a starvation diet.

When Johnson declared that Fielding was inferior to Richardson because he depicted characters of manners and Richardson characters of nature, Boswell thought him singular in his preference, and posterity has agreed with Boswell. The difference of opinion signalizes an historical shift of critical sympathy. Looking back, we can recognize the Great Divide. We do not need to agree with Johnson's rating to realize that the spate of naturalistic data is one consequence of the world's siding with Boswell.

To see *Irene* without prejudice we must retrace our steps and go down the other slope. We must hold before our eyes the vision of a drama wherein we stand upon the vantage ground of Truth—'a hill not to be commanded, and where the air is always clear and serene'. Our private experience is contained there in solution. Everything merely personal, everything irrelevant and insignificant, the dross of casual place and time and circumstance, has been strained off from this thrice repurèd distillation: only the universal remains, and that 'ennobled'. The figures that move in this enchanted world are like animated marble, august or terrible, but dignified and beautiful alike in passion or repose. They speak with a large utterance, as befits their attitudes. They are not gods, but symbols of ourselves, with our thoughts, but more considered; our emotions, but more intense; our words, but richer and more meaningful; our acts, but more deeply significant. There are no impertinent interruptions; no impudent mirthmakers gain admittance. The action is one single co-ordinated impulse, every detail of which has immediate relation to the whole. It is like the arc of a perfect swan dive, or the parabola of a rocket. It is the expression of that animating Simplicity which Collins desiderates as the *sine qua non*:

> Tho' Taste, tho' Genius bless,
> To some divine Excess,
> Faints the cold Work till Thou inspire the whole;
> What each, what all supply,
> May court, may charm, our Eye,
> Thou, only Thou, can'st raise the meeting Soul!

Here is no paltry simulation of fact, but a reality beyond realism.

Such a play, so pure and translucent, with so exquisite a symmetry, so assuaging a beauty, was to be Johnson's *Irene*. But what of Tragedy? What general statement was to be embodied in this perfect form? I do not know that Johnson anywhere set down an analytical definition of tragedy. In his Dictionary he contents himself with a definition that seems to us to omit the essentials of the *genre*: 'A dramatick representation of a serious action'— an inadequacy, however, in which he is followed by the Oxford Dictionary, which merely adds, in its primary definition, 'with a fatal or disastrous conclusion'. To this added requirement Johnson would doubtless for practical purposes have agreed, though not that the word had been or was to be universally so understood. Elsewhere, he says that the 'design of tragedy is to instruct by moving the passions';[21] and thence it could be inferred that such a disastrous conclusion would be most likely to accomplish the end proposed. But to us, nourished as we have been on the commentaries of the last and present centuries, it comes at first with something of a shock to realize how seldom in the last two thousand years tragedy as a literary mode has been received and evaluated in accordance with critical standards which to-day are everywhere regarded as axiomatic. To go at once to the heart of the matter: seldom has *our* sense of the properest way to excite the emotion of pity—fear poses no problem here,—and to resolve it, been acknowledged as the fundamental requirement of true tragedy. We feel, with Aristotle, that there should be a discrepancy in favour of the protagonist between his deserts and his fate, pity being our spontaneous testimony to the fact; and that the resolution of that emotion should reaffirm or restore our sense of an underlying moral or ethical order in the universe, and at the same time vindicate human dignity and worth. As has been recognized before now, the Christian view of existence made it impractical to emphasize the aberration of justice, and devised two evasions of the tragic dilemma. In the one, the re-establishment of order is postponed to another life, while fortune or chance is allowed a comparatively free rein on earth. At the same time, earthly life is relegated to an inferior importance, and the function of pity is no longer paramount. In the alternative scheme, the protagonist's desert tends to be equated with his misfortune, in which case the emotion of pity becomes correspondingly impertinent. When great tragedy is nevertheless achieved, as by Shakespeare, it sidesteps the Christian point of view, and approximates the Greek attitude; or it ostensibly accepts the equation of blame and suffering, and achieves the sense of pity by loading the human value of the individual—thereby, as in the case of *Macbeth*, tacitly denying the equation on another level. Where the Christian viewpoint is squarely faced and accepted, pity must be secured by adventitious means. The tragic key is blunted into the pathetic. But, of course, such a drop may occur through a failure in tragic insight, even when the Christian view is blurred or ignored. And this is the general plight of English tragedy after Shakespeare, as we conceive.

But this is to describe the situation as if our own way of looking at it were absolute and final, instead of the product of a view of the world that has no prescriptive rights for other ages. Just as we are beginning to realize the 'shift in sensibility' (F. A. Pottle's phrase) that blinded us for so long to the presence of emotion in eighteenth-century poetry, so, it may be, we have little right to assume that former generations were unable to recognize and experience the tragic qualm because they rejected Shakespeare's statement of it—as Shakespeare and his contemporaries had in turn rejected earlier statements. If it were only to be evoked from one special formula, there is no reason why, so long as Aristotle was remembered, tragedies upon the classic pattern should not have continued to ennoble the buskined stage. At any rate, it is historical fact that a whole generation, on the Continent as well as in England, thrilled to Addison's *Cato*, a play on which a modern critic, Mr Bonamy Dobrée, after some comments of a realistic sort, can roundly pronounce that 'the whole thing is little short of nauseating'.[22]

Johnson, at any rate, was not disposed to look on human life with an undue amount of lighthearted optimism, nor to brush aside the real ills of it as nugatory or imagined. For him it was 'every where a state in which much is to be endured, and little to be enjoyed'. And it is significant that when he came to estimate the course of tragedy during the century previous to his own, although he recognized a falling off in tragic power, he did not feel that it had been on the wrong road, or that it had lost sight of its proper goal:

> Then crush'd by Rules, and weaken'd as refin'd,
> For Years the Pow'r of Tragedy declin'd;
> From Bard, to Bard, the frigid Caution crept,
> Till Declamation roar'd, while Passion slept.
> Yet still did Virtue deign the Stage to tread,
> Philosophy remain'd, though Nature fled.

Those lines, which contain the charge which Garrick was afterward to quote against *Irene* itself, were written and delivered about a year and a half before *Irene* was heard on the same stage. And they anticipate most of what has been said of it since that day. Thus Mr Allardyce Nicoll:

Declamation dominates *Irene*, sometimes declamation which rises to the height of a grand rhetoric, but declamation will not make a play, so that we remain cold alike at the patriotism of Demetrius and Leontius, the villainy of Cali, the agony of Irene. A frigid chill enwraps the whole work.[23]

But in one of the *Rambler* papers, two years after his play was produced, and three before the second edition of it was demanded, Johnson set down words which are at once a candid criticism of, and an apology for, *Irene* and the whole line in which it stands, indicating the utmost extent of his modest claim:

But though, perhaps, it cannot be pretended that the present age has added much to the force and efficacy of the drama, it has at least been able to escape many faults, which either ignorance had overlooked, or indulgence had licensed. The later tragedies, indeed, have faults of another kind, perhaps more destructive to delight, though less open to censure. That perpetual tumour of phrase with which every thought is now expressed by every personage, the paucity of adventures which regularity admits, and the unvaried equality of flowing dialogue, has taken away from our present writers almost all that dominion over the passions which was the boast of their predecessors. Yet they may at least claim this commendation, that they avoid gross faults, and that if they cannot often move terrour or pity, they are always careful not to provoke laughter.[24]

The commendation has a chilly enough ring, and one is tempted to add a few remarks of more positive compliment. However Johnson may have fallen short of the effect he wished to produce, there was nothing radically wrong with his ideal, and he did not retract it even when he came to praise the triumphs of Shakespeare in an alien kind. The insistence on a special kind of propriety in *Irene* and other members of the same clan, even at great and admitted cost, only means that their age set an extreme value on certain valid artistic satisfactions that other schools of tragedy failed to provide in sufficient measure, and that it was willing to pay the price. Neither were these satisfactions inconsistent with the truth of tragedy.

Of *Irene* in particular, thus much may be said: If Christian ideology is not quite destructive of the tragic principle, the theme upon which it may base its securest defence is that which casts its long shadow beyond the mere term of our present existence, upon the final state of man's immortal soul. The idea of eternal damnation opens to the Christian poet tragic vistas so tremendous as perhaps to dwarf all others of whatever kind. In choosing apostasy as the pivotal theme, Johnson at once lifts his play far above the marsh of the merely pathetic, into which so many Christian tragedies inevitably sink. That he arrived at his chosen theme by an objective process of critical ratiocination I do not for a moment suppose. The idea was terribly real for him, and he was impelled to select it by promptings from the profounder depths of his nature.

From the choice of theme, it follows almost of necessity that the play should have a double issue such as he gives it, and such as Aristotle places in the second rank of excellence. An opposite fate for the good and the bad, according to Aristotle, is sometimes accounted the best plotting, but only 'because of the weakness of the spectators; for the poet is guided', he says, 'by the wishes of his audience'; but the resultant satisfaction 'is not the true tragic pleasure'.[25] But for a Christian poet poetic justice is something more than a concession to an audience's taste; and Johnson could not have confounded Aspasia and Demetrius in a common catastrophe with Irene without destroying the play's significance.

Aside from the double *dénouement*, and taken on its own principles, the plot is very nearly impregnable. It is not because of its construction that the play fails ultimately of success. Fail it certainly does, and I would not be understood to be recommending a reversal of the general verdict. But neither do I believe that it fails on grounds that can be indicated by covering it with that reproachful name, 'pseudoclassical'. I have already said enough to disclose a hearty respect for the ideal which that term obscures rather than designates.

In the end, I suspect—and over and above what has been said earlier of Johnson's untheatrical imagination,—the basic trouble lies in the style. The persons, to be sure, are stiff and insufficiently vitalized. They are so, however, not primarily because of what they do or say, but because of the way in which they say it. The fault is not a mere matter of artificiality of language. It concerns a subtler relationship to living speech, a matter which Mr T. S. Eliot has recently discussed in his W. P. Ker Memorial Lecture at Glasgow (February, 1942). 'No poetry, of course,' he says, 'is ever exactly the same speech that the poet talks and hears: but it has to be in such a relation to the speech of his time that the listener or reader can say "that is how I should talk if I could talk poetry"....[It] must be a music latent in the common speech of its time.' Moreover, he declares, 'the dependence of verse upon speech is much more direct in dramatic poetry than in any other'; and he feels, in regard to the verse plays of the nineteenth century, that 'it is not primarily lack of plot, or lack of action and suspense, or imperfect realization of character, or lack of anything of what is called "theatre", that makes these plays so lifeless: it is primarily that their rhythm of speech is something that we cannot associate with any human being except a poetry reciter'.

To this I should agree, and I would apply his remarks to *Irene*. And I rather suspect that Johnson was partially aware of the same truth in what he had to say of that middle style, to be found in Shakespeare's comedies, which never grows obsolete because it is 'so consonant and congenial' to the language heard in the 'common intercourse of life'. To Johnson it once befell, when the years had detached him sufficiently from his play, to listen to it with the objective ear of a stranger. He was at a country house, and someone was reading *Irene* aloud to the company. After a time, he rose and left the room; 'and somebody having asked him the reason of this, he replied, "Sir, I thought it had been better"'.[26] But the sentiments were the same, the characters and the conduct of the action were the same. What struck him with unpleasant surprise, because he had never really heard it before, was, I am confident, the fact that the style had no roots in the rhythm of speech.

If it were permitted, by way of conclusion, to offer in suggestive summary one of those 'short strictures' such as Johnson made a habit of appending severally to the plays of Shakespeare, the dyer's hand might be found employing the pen to somewhat the following effect:

This tragedy is one of the works upon which our author has apparently laboured; but as success in works of invention is not always proportionate to labour, it is not finished at last with the happy force of some other of his pieces, wherein he seems to have produced without labour, what no labour can improve. It will, perhaps, not often be found that the language of *Irene* exceeds the due bounds of dignified expression, either by extravagant rant, or miserable conceit; but it cannot easily be denied that there is in it a general tumidity of diction that palls upon the ear. Engrossed with the justice of the sentiments, the author appears to have been too little obsequious to the modes of living dialogue. Further acquaintance with the theatre must have made him more apprehensive of the distinction between spoken and written poetry; but of such familiarity the humour of a scholar made him inappetent.

The character of *Demetrius* is conceived with particular sympathy; and in *Aspasia*, a kind of female *Demetrius*, Johnson appears to have taken no common delight. It cannot be maintained that the character of Irene is equally successful. What an author has performed with difficulty and reluctance is unlikely to be perused by his readers with much pleasure. Of the other personages of the drama, nothing particular need be said; they satisfy the requirements of the fable, and no more; yet I know not if that of *Leontius* had not been better excluded. The author's design did not admit of many nice discriminations of character, nor striking delineations of life.

The conduct of the plot is artful, and the unities are exactly observed. It must nevertheless be acknowledged, that had the scenes been busier and more various, and the characters more interestingly diversified, curiosity had been better engaged, and the catastrophe more deeply affecting.

Yet, if the passions are not much aroused by this tragedy, they are at least directed toward their proper end. Morality is enforced and understanding is enlarged by many just sentiments and important truths. To do more than this, I am afraid stands not within the limits of rational expectation.

NOTES

[1] Knolles, *Historie of the Turks*, 1603, p. 350.

[2] *Ibid.* p. 352.

[3] *Ibid.* p. 353.

[4] Such is the bare outline of the central action. But Goring has introduced much original matter along the way. Besides making large provision for musical interludes and spectacle, he has made room for a number of new characters, and quite altered the usual handling of Mahomet's recall to the demands of state. Working behind the scenes is the malevolent figure of the Queen Mother, a virago identified merely as the Sultana Validé in the cast of characters but calling herself Despina in the final scene. She may probably have been developed from Roxelana, appearing in Knolles, pp. 759–760, as the favorite wife of Solyman the Magnificent, *circa* 1552. The Sultana incites Mahomet's malicious Grand Vizier to ply the outspoken general, Balbanus (according to Knolles, Balabanus was Mahomet's general against Scanderbeg at the siege of Croia, where he was killed; cf. pp. 400 ff.), and the loyal Acmet Bassa with wine at the Byram Feast. The scheme works, and black mantles are thrown over the offenders in token of the death sentence. (These elements are derived from Knolles' account of Baiazet's treatment of Achmetes, in 1484; cf. p. 443. But Johnson may have taken the black mantle straight from Goring.) Mustapha asks to be included with his friends in the death penalty. In the prison scene that follows, Mahomet overhears the conversation of the three friends, loyal to himself, and thereupon forgives their presumption at the banquet.

[5] At one point Goring tries to foreshadow the *dénouement*. In his heated slumber, Mahomet dreams that he has stabbed Irene, and wakes to find blood on his sword. He learns, however, that in drink he has slain a favourite eunuch, and he now deplores having broken the sacred law.

[6] Swinhoe occasionally employs blank verse, but writes mostly in cadenced prose, or a very free verse. The version of 1664 is in cadenced prose and occasional couplets.

[7] *The Poems of Samuel Johnson*, ed. D. Nichol Smith and E. L. McAdam, Oxford, 1941, p. 237.

[8] Translated by Knolles:

If feature braue thou doest respect, thou canst none fairer see,
    Nor in whose chast and constant brest could greater graces
      lie.
But whilst mismatcht she liu'd to mourne, enthrald to jealous
    braine,
    Vnhappie she, with cruell hand was by her husband slaine.

The portraits and verses are on pp. 558–559 of the *Historie*.

[9] Knolles, 1603, p. 557.

[10] I have subsequently noted that Baker's *Biographia Dramatica*, III, 331, mentions the likelihood that Johnson may have taken hints from this play.

[11] This is not quite accurate. A recently recovered manuscript notebook, now in the Hyde Collection, contains twelve pages of notes and draft speeches for *Irene*, Act V. These are printed in the new edition of Johnson's *Poems*, ed. E. L. McAdam, Jr. with George Milne, Yale University Press, New Haven and London, 1964, pp. 229–236. The speeches appear to post-date those in the BM manuscript.

[12] See especially, on this question, the extremely penetrating and careful section III in Josephine Miles, *Wordsworth and the Vocabulary of Emotion*, Univ. Calif. Publ. English, Vol. 12, No. 1 (1942).

[13] Boswell, *Life of Johnson*, Hill-Powell ed. I, 73–74.

[14] *Life*, I, 80.

[15] *Life*, I, 454.

[16] *The Idler*, No. 89. *Works*, 1825 ed., IV, 413.

[17] *Life*, III, 339.

[18] *Life*, I, 95.

[19] Cf. *Life*, I, 100 ff.

[20] *Letters*, ed. G. B. Hill, I, 3–6.

[21] *The Rambler*, No. 156.

[22] *Restoration Tragedy*, 1929, p. 175.

[23] *History of Early Eighteenth Century Drama*, 1925, p. 95.

[24] *The Rambler*, No. 125, May 28, 1751. Works, 1825 ed. III, 97–98.

[25] *Poetics*, XIII, 7 (Butcher's trans.).

[26] *Life*, IV, 5.

THE DOUBLE TRADITION
OF DR. JOHNSON

In a sense so deep as to give most of its meaning to the study of literary history, a great writer is defined not only by his own works but also by what posterity makes of him. What he has meant to the generations between his own and ours is an essential part of what he comes to mean to us. After his death there springs up an eidolon of an author, and it is of this everchanging surrogate, not of the original, that we inevitably form our judgments, and that by so judging we further change. Every such image is an instance of one sort of literary tradition, and, like all tradition, a continuity. Let the losses or gains, the changes, reversals, or accretions be what they may, there can be no second beginning. Every phase of the tradition is an immediate consequence. The original, moreover, is forever inaccessible, and, were it not so, that original would still not be the truth. For the truth is always becoming: the truth of living tradition neither was, nor is, nor shall be, but exists in a continuum. Absolute judgments of a literary figure, therefore, can never possess more than a momentary and private validity, since the eidolon upon which they base themselves is never long the same. Whether consciously or not, we are all necessarily students of tradition in being students of literature. And this would appear to be equally true whether we study the work of a man or a man in his work. It is to this aspect of tradition—not the operative power of tradition which we denominate influence, but something more akin to a transmitted recollection, to a song or ballad—that present attention is invited.

These remarks are to focus in Dr. Johnson, and by

implication I have raised the question whether it is possible for two people, or for two generations, to remember and discuss the same Dr. Johnson. The problem of Johnson's identity is further complicated by circumstances almost, if not quite, unique. The uniqueness lies, of course, in the fact that it is possible to 'know' this man, in his habit as he lived, as intimately as we can 'know' his works. The fullness of the biographical record is without parallel for any comparable figure. (Boswell is an exception, but Boswell is incomparable.)

Hence, Johnson has come down to us in a double tradition. Like any other author, he exists for us in his works. But he exists for us also like a character in one of our older novels, and on the same level of objectivity and familiarity. The traditional personality began to be shaped before his death, but became condensed and fully substantiated in Boswell's *Tour* and *Life*. The descent of the two traditions, of the personality and of the author—which we shall differentiate for convenience as the popular and the learned traditions—has proceeded neither with equal stability nor along a parallel track. The popular tradition has been much less affected by the refreshing or contaminating influences of print.

Every student of oral tradition knows that the approved method of procedure is to stop your carrier where you meet him, note the place and date, put questions, get him to talk, and take down his report verbatim. To reach a relatively accurate definition of Johnson as he exists today in popular tradition, one ought to collect as many variants as possible from representative cultural levels and areas, collate and analyze the data, find the common core, trace the deviations and 'sports', detect the lines of transmission, and establish the norm in the popular mind of the time. The research would be expensive and time-consuming, and I doubt if it has ever been proposed to a Foundation as a proper project for subsidy. Nevertheless, we might learn a good deal from such an investigation about the ways of tradition, the shaping of popular myth, about the nature and component elements of a literary persona abstracted from whatever sources and abraded by the ebb and flow of collective memory. Without it, we can only guess at the state and distribution of the tradition here prefigured.

At its feeblest, the popular tradition is probably little more than an eponym for a crushing reply. In its middling state, it is usually the object of affectionate regard, seldom of opprobrium. What we should doubtless find most frequently in the folk-image would be the ideas of physical bulk, sloppy habits of dress, bad manners, loud voice, witty but weighty speech. There would be a general notion of a man who was always saying quotable things and who had written books that nobody read. In fuller variants, examples of his good things would be cited; and doubtless in the books of Familiar Quotations we should find the likeliest instances of his repartee. Johnson's animal farm would show itself: at the very least, the Cow, the Bull, and the Dog, in those unsuitable postures wherein he delighted to show them for analogical consideration.

The popular image thus faintly and imperfectly suggested would not, we feel sure, have perpetuated itself in the common memory for so long, had Boswell not done his work with such unexampled vividness. But Boswell's image was of a complexity and subtlety far transcending what could be used and carried by the general. Cheap and striking reproduction, enormously simplified, was the need; and the need was supplied, unquestionably, by Macaulay's review of Croker's *Boswell*, in 1831. Macaulay has dropped his seine into Boswell's waters and drawn up nearly all the details that have persisted in later popular variants. He tumbles them headlong into one sprawling sentence:

DOUBLE TRADITION OF DR. JOHNSON

Everything about him, his coat, his wig, his figure, his face, his scrofula, his St. Vitus's dance, his rolling walk, his blinking eye, the outward signs which too clearly marked his approbation of his dinner, his insatiable appetite for fish-sauce and veal-pie with plums, his inextinguishable thirst for tea, his trick of touching the posts as he walked, his mysterious practice of treasuring up scraps of orange-peel, his morning slumbers, his midnight disputations, his contortions, his mutterings, his gruntings, his puffings, his vigorous, acute, and ready eloquence, his sarcastic wit, his vehemence, his insolence, his fits of tempestuous rage, his queer inmates, old Mr. Levett and blind Mrs. Williams, the cat Hodge and the negro Frank, all are as familiar to us as the objects by which we have been surrounded from childhood.

For every statement of a traditional theme that has the fortune to be written down, there are thousands that go unrecorded. But we have to plot the course of tradition in the individual versions that achieve the accidental permanence of print. Macaulay's essay of 1856 shows variations such as one might note in the rendition of a ballad by the same singer a quarter of a century later. Some parts drop out, others come into stronger prominence: in this case, the later version is softer and more kindly. The variation is so slight, however, as rather to reinforce Macaulay's influence on the popular tradition than to modify it. This second essay, reprinted countless times in school editions, is that which has made it unnecessary for all but the curious and the scholarly-minded ever to read Boswell. 'The old philosopher', it concludes unforgettably, 'is still among us in the brown coat with the metal buttons and the shirt which ought to be at wash, blinking, puffing, rolling his head, drumming with his fingers, tearing his meat like a tiger, and swallowing his tea in oceans.' The imago is now fixed as firmly as such things can be. (Imago, says the ACD, is 'an idealized concept of a loved one, formed in childhood and retained uncorrected in adult life.')

DOUBLE TRADITION OF DR. JOHNSON

Carlyle's version, put on paper in 1832 partly to offset Macaulay, preferable in some respects though it is, seems to have had little effect on the popular idea. It is too idiosyncratically conceived and expressed to find familiar residence in the common mind. Carlyle deliberately sets about making a myth, turning the man Johnson into a personified abstraction. Illustrative of the technique is a brief passage describing Johnson as a college student:

A rugged wild-man of the desert, awakened to the feeling of himself; proud as the proudest, poor as the poorest; stoically shut up, silently enduring the incurable: what a world of blackest gloom, with sun-gleams and pale tearful moon-gleams, and flickerings of a celestial and an infernal splendour, was this that now opened for him! But the weather is wintry; and the toes of the man are looking through his shoes. His muddy features grow of a purple and sea-green colour; a flood of black indignation mantling beneath.

Regarded as a variant in the series, this is too far from the traditional norm: it has been contaminated by the concept of Hero as Man of Letters.

At this point let us turn from the popular to that other branch, which I have called the learned, tradition. What we are to observe is the eidolon, continually remoulded, successively and responsibly viewed in Johnson's works and in the light of all that can be known about him. Every stage of the process is contiguous upon the precedent one; and it is this awareness, and not congruity of opinion, that constitutes the continuity inherent in the idea of tradition.

All description of the learned tradition must falsify by oversimplification. Even to his contemporaries Johnson presented contrary faces; but broadly speaking the man and his works then appeared commensurate, were of a piece, and were great. Separation probably began before the end of the century, and was doubtless hastened by the appearance of Boswell's *Life*. But in 1817 it was still possible for Alexander Chalmers to declare: 'the world has agreed ... to rank him among the most illustrious writers of any age or nation, and among the benefactors to religion, virtue, and learning.' Of *The Rambler* in particular: 'since the work became popular, every thing in literature or morals, in history or dissertation, is better conceived, and better expressed—conceived with more novelty, and expressed with greater energy.'

In another twenty years, however, the cleavage has become so marked that Macaulay can unquestioningly give the palm to the Johnson in Boswell, a 'far greater' figure than Johnson the author. Says Macaulay:

His conversation appears to have been quite equal to his writings in matter, and far superior to them in manner ... As soon as he took his pen in his hand to write for the public, his style became systematically vicious ... It is clear that Johnson himself did not think in the dialect in which he wrote. The expressions which came first to his tongue were simple, energetic, and picturesque. When he wrote for publication, he did his sentences out of English into Johnsonese. (Further:) His whole code of criticism rested on pure assumption. (And again:) The characteristic peculiarity of his intellect was the union of great powers with low prejudices.

The lectures of Thomas Sergeant Perry, published 1882 under the title, *English Literature in the Eighteenth Century*, show us the learned tradition apparently by that time immutably set along the lines forecast by Macaulay. This was authoritative opinion, careful and conscientious, abreast of Continental as well as English and American scholarship. With the confidence of learning and leadership, Perry declared of Johnson: that all his views had been riddled by later opinion, that *The Rambler* was unreadable, like a petrifaction of Addison and Steele; that, while it might be allowed that the Preface to Shakespeare, though tinged with antique notions, had been serviceable to letters, the influence of the Lives of the Poets could only have been bad. Yet it was not enough to say of him merely that he had encouraged philistinism. 'With all his faults, he is one of the best-loved men in the history of letters, and this is due, not to his writings, but to the faithful record' etc. 'Dr. Johnson's reputation, then, is due to Boswell's book.' So powerful was the tradition by this time that even Leslie Stephen, capable of understanding Johnson and sympathetic to him at many points, deprecates his writing. 'Johnson's sentences', he writes, 'seem to be contorted, as his gigantic limbs used to twitch, by a kind of mechanical spasmodic action.' 'And yet', he faintly pleads for *The Rambler*, 'with all its faults, the reader who can plod through its pages will at least feel respect for the author.'

As early as the first decade of the new century there were outspoken protests against the prevailing view. In his historical anthology of English Prose, Henry Craik makes a vigorous attack upon what he calls 'the parody which lives in the popular estimation'. He stands uncompromisingly for Johnson as an author, and declares that, 'in style alone, we may justly claim that he is the vertebrate column of our prose'. Craik brings us back to a view of Johnson surprisingly close to that of Chalmers a century before: 'it is not too much', he goes on, 'to say that all that is best in English prose since his day is his debtor in respect of not a few of its highest qualities'; and of the *Lives of the Poets* he states his conviction that, 'for vigour and ease and variety of style, for elasticity of confidence, for keenness of sarcasm, for brightness of humour, the *Lives* hold the first place, absolutely free from competition, amongst all works of English criticism of similar range.'

Taken as a whole, Craik's praise, during the present half-century, and within what I have called the learned tradition, has not yet been reversed. Rather, reinforced immediately by the brilliant essays of Walter Raleigh, it has become in its turn the accepted view, and has been elaborated and refined upon by an impressive and growing number of discriminating scholar-critics.

It is true that tradition is embodied only in its individual instances, is ultimately the sum of these manifestations. There is no instrumentality that will reconcile incommensurables or reduce the prismatic rays of tradition to 'the wide effulgence of a summer noon'. But if we are not to give over our allotted space to a gallery talk among the portraits of Dr. Johnson, we must try to put together some kind of composite that will display his features with the emphases characteristic of our understanding of him. When we look for the points where Johnson's thought seems to focus with maximum intensity, we find them where the currents of his day, whether political, religious, or literary, are threatening to break over into channels leading, as he thought, to mischievous ends. We find them where he is most stoutly engaged in resisting these tendencies. This resistance goes under the name of Johnson's conservatism, and it is by a closer and more sympathetic examination of its character and quality that we find our view of Johnson diverging most sharply from older tradition.

Conservatism is a chameleon term that gets most of its meaning from its surroundings. It can have a negative, a neutral, or a positive cast. It may mean a dogged reluctance to surrender private or group advantage; it may mean a lazy habit of mind that dislikes any change; it may mean a passionate and aggressive determination to preserve the best. Thus, Churchill was heroically conservative in 1942. In 1946, to many, he was a reactionary. So far as we can tell, he and his principles remained unaltered. Conservatism is certainly no genuine opposite to progressivism, unless the latter be carelessly taken as a spirit of innovation.

When conservatism is the position of a small minority, it sometimes acquires a radical look. Thus, Rousseau has lately been described—and with justice—as a violent reactionary, sick with nostalgia for an imaginary past where man had lived free and exquisitely uncivilized, barbarously refined.

Of late we have come to perceive more clearly that the spirit that animated Johnson, in his maturity as in his early years, was a positive, not a negative nor a neutral, spirit. The youth of whom he allows us retrospective glimpses in his later conversation was a being very restive under the restraints of his environment, and forward to propose iconoclastic if hypothetical improvements. Between the ages of 25 and 35, he was a violent and outspoken opponent of the government and the reigning house:—a homeless, penniless, dangerous man, keeping questionable company, tramping the streets all night for lack of a lodging or money to pay for one; sustained by political passion, 'brimful of patriotism', 'resolved to stand by his country' by writing incendiary anti-ministerial pamphlets; the misreporter of Parliamentary debates and, in fact, wanted for questioning by the authorities. Temperamentally intemperate, he was yet less disreputable than would appear, for his passion was supported then and thenceforward by convictions about the bases and structure of society, and of man's obligations to God and his fellowman which ultimately confirmed his service under the banner of Law.

Macaulay was right when he called him 'as a politician, half ice and half fire'; but Macaulay, it now appears, was quite wrong in the sense he gave to his own remark. For Macaulay thought him, in politics, intellectually apathetic and passionate from unfounded prejudice; and considered that the notorious conversation with Sir Adam Fergusson was enough to demonstrate Johnson's gross and palpable illogicality. For in one breath Johnson could say, 'I would not give half a guinea to live under one form of government rather than another'; and in the next, could turn on his opponent with the outburst, 'Sir, I perceive you are a vile Whig.'

To correct Macaulay, we must look a little more inquiringly into this *volte face*. The scene took place at the Pantheon, where, it will be recalled, Sir Adam 'expressed some apprehension' lest such public amusements might encourage luxury in the populace. Luxury, he declared, 'corrupts a people and destroys the spirit of liberty'. Johnson, as we know, thought that the mass of the common people was in very little immediate danger from overabundance of material delights, and always protested at their being denied any innocent sweeteners of a bitter existence. 'Luxury', he said, 'so far as it reaches the poor, will do good to the race of people; it will strengthen and multiply them.' He therefore put by Sir Adam's philosophical cant with a common-sense answer: 'Sir, I am a great friend to publick amusements; for they keep people from vice.' Pressed again on the theoretical ground—the fear that the spirit of liberty would be sapped—he declared, 'Sir, that is all visionary.' Setting aside the fact that the threat of epidemic luxury was non-existent, where was the national emergency that demanded that the nation be kept on the alert to preserve its liberty? No foreign power was menacing. But Sir Adam, it appeared, was afraid of the encroachments of the King's Party. Johnson maintained that the average Briton was likely to feel very little effect in his private life, whatever the temporary complexion of Parliament. If the country remained peaceful, even a monarchy in the old sense permitted the normal freedoms of daily living, which were all that the common subject was aware of. 'Liberty', he had written some twenty years earlier, 'is, to the lowest rank of every nation, little more than the choice of working or starving; and this choice is, I suppose, equally allowed in every country.' If ordinary men were to be denied amusements lest they grow slack and be unable to put up resistance to a danger which even if fully realized they would not feel, what a coil was here! At such a distance from immediate experience, the form of government itself made little difference. 'But, Sir', insisted Sir Adam, 'in the British Constitution it is surely of importance to keep up a spirit in the people, so as to preserve a balance against the Crown.' JOHNSON. 'Sir, I perceive you are a vile Whig. Why all this childish jealousy of the power of the crown? The crown has not power enough. When I say that all governments are alike, I consider that in no government power can be abused long. Mankind will not bear it. If a sovereign oppresses his people to a great degree, they will rise and cut off his head. There is a remedy in human nature against tyranny, that will keep us safe under every form of government.'

Behind Johnson's impatient assertion that the Crown had not power enough, was the theory, most clearly expressed in *Taxation No Tyranny*, that the stability of a society rested on the presence in it somewhere of an impartial, absolute authority, above challenge, to which all contestants could appeal. In the British system, the king was the embodiment of this principle, the symbol of an ultimate authority, the idea of decisive right. If, as man, he descended from that high level, his political defects or perversive influence on the operation of justice and wisdom in the State—a possibility which Johnson readily admitted —could be checked or resisted in the persons of his ministers. 'Redress is always to be had against oppression, by punishing the immediate agents.' In effect, then, his subjects would be appealing from him as fallible man to his idea as King infallible. Analogies with the Church are obvious here and need not be developed. Johnson wished that there might be as close an approximation as possible between the king in person and the King as Principle. The Whig effort, on the contrary, was to separate the two by reducing the actual authority of the king and by denying the absolute authority of Sovereignty. Their work, therefore, was ultimately the undermining and destruction of all authority in the State except that of temporary power. Hence Johnson called Whiggism the negation of principle, and declared that the first Whig was the Devil. On the ground of theory, therefore, his retort to Sir Adam involved his whole political philosophy: it was not from pique but from principle. But in the other, the practical, context, he was not inconsistent in saying that the danger of the abuse of power was nothing to a private man, and that the form of government made little difference to the happiness of the individual. His proviso, of course, is essential: that if the actual sovereign grows outrageous, and the abuse becomes enormous, humanity will reestablish its rights by overturning the corrupt system ... It is impossible to grant the justice here of Macaulay's accusation of an implicit logical dilemma.

Doubtless, there are inconsistencies, and paradoxes in the texture of Johnson's thought and speech, and they are no small part of its perennial interest. His sense of moral responsibility has always been recognized. But we see more distinctly today his deep intellectual responsibility as well; and no careful student will now accuse him seriously of setting up thoughtless prejudices in lieu of principles, even where his pronouncements seem to us most cross-grained and perverse.

It is ironically unjust that Johnson should have come to typify, in so many minds, a stubborn resistance to change. The group of whom such a charge could be most fairly made were those inglorious Whigs of his day who were most of all concerned, not to defend principle, but to hold fast to the advantages and emoluments of which they and their friends had become possessed half a century and more ago, and who were motivated in the main by little better than indolent self-interest. They *were* conservative, in a sense that cannot properly be used of Johnson: and he despised them because they were *bottomless*. They were quasi-Tories when in place, but without the underlying philosophy of conservatism, and therefore fundamentally dishonest. He fought them as he fought other kinds of dishonesty, with such tools as he found at hand.

Unquestionably, Johnson's political philosophy was deeply rooted in his religion. The stability of the State, the principle of authority in the State, derived its patent from the Supreme Authority above all states, which governed, however inscrutably, by the moral law adumbrated in the Christian revelation and doctrine. But now, as to our knowledge and understanding of Johnson's religion, it appears to me that we are scarcely more enlightened than were our great-grandparents—if indeed we have not moved farther away from the very possibility of understanding. Nothing of genuine consequence, at any rate, has appeared in print upon the subject. We read the Prayers and Meditations and are moved by the spectacle of Johnson's emotion. We stand respectfully by while he and Boswell discuss theology—or we may prefer to wait outside till they have finished. We read with mild interest and approval the sermons he penned for Dr. Taylor—or more probably we never look at them. We do look, and with sympathetic awe, at the occasional manifestations of his religious terror. But few of us indeed can follow him to the depths of his self-abasement; and those who try are likely to emerge with an untidy little parcel of sciolism insecurely wrapped in pseudo-scientific verbiage. Hypothesis may be tested by experience, but is no substitute for experience. What we seem to observe is a spirit profoundly troubled, not so visibly by religious doubts as by religious convictions. Johnson does not allow us to see him questioning his Maker, but only questioning himself, in order to condemn himself. It may be that this is the only sensible and decent attitude: at any rate, Johnson, in spite of his piety and devotion and genuine religious need, seems very seldom to have received much comfort or happiness from his Christian faith. It is symptomatic that he protested against Blair's assertion that the man 'who does not feel joy in religion is far from the kingdom of heaven'. 'There are many good men', Johnson insisted, 'whose fear of God predominates over their love.' He admitted to having been a sceptic in early life; but in the years when we know him best seems not often to have been troubled with serious difficulty of that kind. Yet it may be guessed that the act of believing where he could not rationally prove ran counter to his inmost nature. He once wrote: 'None would have recourse to an invisible power, but that all other subjects have eluded their hopes.' He clung to his faith because he was determined to *believe* only because he could not prove, and because he regarded the alternatives of unbelief or agnosticism as doctrines of utter abandoned despair. It seems just to say that he had to believe in the truth of the Christian revelation or lose his sanity; for on that anchor, for him, entirely depended the meaning of existence.

Noting Johnson's extreme habitual scepticism, Macaulay nevertheless charges him with the grossest credulity and downright superstition. 'It is curious', he writes, 'to observe . . . the contrast between the disdainful manner in which he rejects unauthenticated anecdotes, even when they are consistent with the general laws of nature, and the respectful manner in which he mentions the wildest stories relating to the invisible world.' But the paradox is not a paradox when we understand that it was the sceptical habit of mind, requiring rational demonstration of what he *had* to believe, that drove him to personal investigation of all reports of the supernatural. Not superstition, but the opposite. To the question, Were not the evidences of Christianity sufficient? he replied, 'Yes, but I would have more.'

In fact, Johnson's orthodoxy can be taken as one more evidence of that *un*conservative spirit we divine in him, of the strength of his temperamental bias, to inquire, and try, and prove all things. It was the strait-jacket, or at least the curb and the tight rein, that he felt it necessary to impose upon himself. It was the sign of his self-distrust, a tacit confession of his radical intemperance, the intellectual counterpart of that physical intemperance which so struck Boswell: 'Every thing about his character and manners was forcible and violent; there never was any moderation ... He could practise abstinence, but not temperance.'

It is this pervasive sense of what Johnson is keeping in leash, of energy not allowed to run wild, but controlled only by determined and unremitting effort, that makes the man so fascinating. When we look closely, we see that his conservatism vibrates like a taut wire. The immobility that to the casual eye has sometimes appeared to be the mere rigidity of moribund attitudes is now seen to be the precarious triumph of self-government. In days when all fundamental values are subjected to continual challenge, we can look with especial sympathy on one who fought so strenuously not to destroy but to hold fast that which was good.

The spectacle would be interesting even if we found nothing of value in what Johnson was attempting to preserve. But, thanks to Time's whirligig, we now see much that may stead us in our own need, or the challenge of which may serve for measure and clarification of our principles. And nowhere more readily, perhaps, than in confirming literary standards.

Basically, the question of Johnson's value as poet and critic turns on the antinomy of the Particular and the General. It is sufficiently obvious that the nineteenth-century hatred of eighteenth-century poetry was at bottom a hatred of abstraction. Equally clear is the fact that the great triumphs of the nineteenth century were won in important degree by keeping the eye on the object and describing it, however small, however particular, however individualized. By shifting the center of reference from the human race to the human individual, the scale of relative values is violently altered. To move out of the eighteenth century into the nineteenth is an experience like passing from the first book of Gulliver's Travels into the second, where every one is a giant. The Ego becomes the measure of all things.

As Gulliver found out, it is hard to get used to a different scale from the one in which we have been nurtured. The scale of the nineteenth century revealed the strangeness of the world of minutiae and carried with it all the excitements of a voyage into the unknown. The normative values of the eighteenth century were so tame by comparison as hardly to stir the most languid interest. And if the poetry was so dull, it must follow that the criticism supporting that dullness was equally dull, unenlightened, and misguided.

It was only when the celebration of the ego had nearly destroyed any binding frame of general reference and the crowded mass of naturalistic detail had created a scene without perspective, where everything appeared to claim equal importance:—only then did it begin to be asked once more whether individualism was always and invariably good, and whether older ways of conveying truth in art might not have some validity. It became possible to inquire whether the giants of the nineteenth century were really any bigger than the giants of the eighteenth century, or whether perhaps they were after all only giants through a microscope.

Johnson's criticism began to be consulted afresh, and it was found that his judgment of the 'metaphysical' poets had considerable bearing upon the current indigestion. 'If', he wrote,

> that be considered as wit which is at once natural and new, that which, though not obvious, is, upon its first production, acknowledged to be just; if it be that which he that never found it, wonders how he missed; to wit of this kind the metaphysical poets have seldom risen. Their thoughts are often new, but seldom natural; they are not obvious, but neither are they just, and the reader, far from wondering that he missed them, wonders more frequently by what perverseness of industry they were ever found . . .
> . . . they never attempted that comprehension and expanse of thought which at once fills the whole mind, and of which the first effect is sudden astonishment, and the second rational admiration . . . Great thoughts are always general, and consist in positions not limited by exceptions, and in descriptions not descending to minuteness.

This very familiar passage has been quoted, not to compel assent, but because it is a masterly statement of a critical position inveterately and fundamentally hostile to what has proved to be the subsequent course of English poetry, a position to which the dilemma of modern verse has given an urgency quite lacking at its first utterance. It is plain, moreover, that Johnson is not here opposing the unknown because he is afraid of it, nor because he is sentimentally fond of the old and familiar, but because he believes essential values are better achieved by one route than by another.

To defend the eighteenth-century position does not fall

within my present purpose. I am the less concerned to do so because it is common knowledge that during the last few decades there has occurred so major a reorientation of critical sympathy and judgment that today it is the Romantics, not their immediate elders, who are most likely to need defense. In sympathetic response, no doubt, to the deeper temper of our generation, a multitude of zealous workers has been laboring in the eighteenth-century vineyard, and this cultivation has quite transformed the quality of the grape. The vintage is a good deal headier than it used to be, and it were not surprising if some of us, soul-hydroptic, were over-exhilarated.

What is at any rate indisputable is the shift in our vision of Johnson which manifests itself when we turn to almost any standard history of English literature written in our time and compare it with those of the previous generation. So far as concerns the 'learned tradition', the eidolon has been quite re-formed.

But it remains to inquire whether there has been a comparable alteration of the popular image, and whether in fact the work of devoted specialists has made any impact on general opinion. It might be presumed that the literate public at least would be affected; but it appears likely that the folk-image still persists on a far higher level of culture than the specialist would ever dream possible. Even among the teaching profession, almost certainly on the lower levels, and perhaps also at the upper ones where specialization in other areas of literary study has prevented reconsideration, the Macaulayan simulacrum probably yet prevails.

Substance accrues to these suspicions in the shape of two books published within the last four years, one entitled *Ursa Major*, by C. E. Vulliamy, the other, *The Conversations of Dr. Johnson*, edited by Raymond Postgate. Mr. Vulliamy has been engaged for more than a decade upon a private crusade against the eighteenth century, in the course of which he has singled out as objects of his special vengeance several of the Johnsonian circle. Boswell and Mrs. Thrale have each been victimized in a book apiece, and lastly the Bear himself has become the special target of Mr. Vulliamy's hostility. This venomous attack has perhaps received as much critical notice as it deserves, but it demands our attention because it displays in a form somewhat distorted by superior knowledge the old imago suggested by the nickname and promoted by Macaulay. Mr. Vulliamy, doubtless, has read all the relevant material, including the writings of Johnson himself. He declares, in fact, that Johnson is 'only to be appreciated by those who grimly undertake the study of his writings.' His own grim study helps him to the content of a final chapter, in which he illustrates how wrong Johnson was in how many ways. Although he qualifies Macaulay's portrait with added charity for the best of Johnson's prose, he quotes as 'incontrovertibly true' the 'just and simple words' of the 1831 essay: 'The characteristic peculiarity of his intellect was the union of great powers with low prejudices.' Vulliamy concludes that 'Johnson was a bully and a snob', who hated new ideas as he did immersion in a bath, who stood for convention because it was conventional, and who fascinates the timid because they admire mere pugnacity. He ends his book on the note of satire, with a quoted passage in short couplets concluding as follows:

> For Mr. Johnson won't allow
> That any but himself can know
> The mysteries of high dispute,
> Where noise, not sense, is absolute,
> And every argument is drown'd
> In roaring tides of angry sound.

Yet on this same final page he has already recommended the study of Johnson's writings, albeit grimly, has even promised some rich and unexpected rewards for the pains, has mentioned Johnson's 'sturdy mind' and 'honest virtues', and declared that he could stand clear of Boswell upon his own merits. *Timeo Danaos.* Such a labefactation of principle who can uphold?

Mr. Postgate's book is a very different kind of work. The body of it, filling 300 pages, consists of Boswell's record of Johnson's conversation, strained out of the *Life* with as little other matter as possible. The operation has an exceptional, if unintended, interest, because it shows as nothing else could do how essentially Boswell's biographical art of disposition and proportion, of anticipatory explanation and skilful highlighting, of balance and perspective, has contributed to the greatness of his book. But our special and immediate interest lies in Mr. Postgate's introductory matter: a brief preface and a biographical sketch of Johnson up to the time when he met Boswell. The point of view of the sketch is nearly identical with that of Macaulay, who seems in fact to have been under the eye of the author as he wrote. There are the same emphases, the same details, the same judgments: Johnson tore his food at table because he had picked up bad habits while living in filth and misery. His wife was, to quote Macaulay, a 'raddled grandmother'. His *Shakespeare*, to quote Macaulay, 'added nothing to the fame of his abilities and learning'. His *Rambler*, to quote Macaulay, is written in Johnsonese. His 'mind was limited'. 'He was not only a Tory, he was that peculiarly immovable and disastrous Tory who really believes that all forms of government are almost equally bad.' 'His *Dictionary* has long ago been superseded, his *Shakespeare* is never consulted, very few people open the files of *The Rambler*, or *The Idler*, his verse is neglected, *Rasselas* unread, and it is chiefly students who still turn to his *Lives of the Poets*. . . . 'It is only by his conversations that Johnson is remembered.' We perceive that Mr. Postgate is little better than a vile Whig.

But how can we sufficiently admire the vitality of this folk-image? It captures the imagination of generation after generation; it takes possession of some minds to such an extent that they spend years reading about Johnson and his circle, and even publish their own books on him, and all the while before them looms the same imago, unabashed and incorrigible. It is a humbling spectacle and a chastening one to the specialist. Each of us brings his burnt offering to the altar of truth, and the figure we invoke becomes momentarily visible, obscurely forming and re-forming in the smoke above us, never the same. But the folk-image moves irresistibly onward, almost unaffected by our puny efforts to arrest or divert it.

> We do it wrong, being so majestical,
> To offer it the show of violence;
> For it is, as the air, invulnerable,
> And our vain blows malicious mockery.